Sweet Dreams

Reversible Quilts and Coordinates

PAMELA LINDQUIST

Martingale™
& C O M P A N Y

Sweet Dreams: Reversible Quilts and Coordinates
©2002 Pamela Lindquist

Martingale & Company
20205 144th Avenue NE
Woodinville, WA 98072-8478
www.martingale-pub.com

Printed in China
07 06 05 04 03 02   8 7 6 5 4 3 2 1

Library of Congress Cataloging-in-Publication Data
Lindquist, Pamela
     Sweet dreams: reversible quilts and coordinates /
Pamela Lindquist.
          p. cm.
     ISBN 1-56477-428-7
     1. Patchwork—Patterns. 2. Quilting—Patterns.
3. Coverlets. 4. Pillows. I. Title.
TT835 .L53 2002
746.46'041—dc21
                                        2002011798

Credits

President: Nancy J. Martin
CEO: Daniel J. Martin
Publisher: Jane Hamada
Editorial Director: Mary V. Green
Managing Editor: Tina Cook
Technical Editor: Ellen Pahl
Copy Editor: Karen Koll
Design and Production Manager: Stan Green
Illustrator: Robin Strobel
Cover Designer: Stan Green
Text Designer: Regina Girard
Photographer: Brent Kane

Acknowledgements

My heartfelt thanks and appreciation go first of all to my mother and father who believed that kids learn by doing and provided me with plenty of hands-on experiences. Thank you to my many friends who listened to my ideas and told me to go for it. For the wonderful machine quilting designs that enhance the quilts in this book, my thanks go to professional quilter Kris Bizzarri. I also want to acknowledge and thank my children, Nathan and Sarah, for their appreciation of quilts and their patience while I wrote this book. And my dear husband, Rick, has always encouraged me with his words and example to look for new adventures and blaze new trails.

Mission Statement
We are dedicated to providing quality products and service by working together to inspire creativity and to enrich the lives we touch.

Contents

Stars Ensemble

Floral Baskets Ensemble

Rose Garden Ensemble

Preface

In my family, we grew up with quilts—not the meticulously pieced and beautifully hand-quilted heirloom quilts that you see at state fairs and quilt shows, but quilts that you would take to the ballpark or to the beach. As a child, I remember carefully cutting leftover fabric scraps from homemade dresses and curtains into 6" squares. I would then practice sewing straight seams with my mother's sewing machine as I joined the squares to each other. I paired calicos with plaids and placed stripes next to polka dots. It really didn't seem to matter since it was a scrap quilt, something made out of leftovers. But for me, it was the beginning of a lifelong interest that has provided me with endless hours of creativity and entertainment.

On my wedding day, my father, a man of few words, took my husband-to-be aback by sharing what he must have perceived as one of my greatest virtues. His words to my husband: "She won't spend your money. You know why? Because she's frugal; you know where she gets that? Me." I relate this story because my dad was right. Let's just say that as a quilter, I am not one to waste fabric.

When I first began making quilts I used a bed sheet for the backing. Once I graduated to actually buying yardage, I often found myself short of fabric to cover the back entirely. I realized that when it came time to buy fabric for the quilt backing I would try to buy the least amount possible, and sometimes I underestimated. I think subconsciously that it was hard for me to spend the money on expensive fabric "just to cover the back" when no one would see it. When I did run short, rather than buy more fabric, I would go through my stash and add strips or panels. This gave the impression, to non-quilters at least, that I had planned these "additions." After a while, I found that this added piecing made the quilt backing not only more affordable, but also more interesting.

From that point on, I decided I would rather buy more of the fabrics used in the quilt top and combine them in a fun way with leftover fabrics from my stash. I realized that I was actually piecing two quilts together for the price of one. I challenged myself to keep my costs down but found that I also enjoyed the process of planning and piecing the quilt backing. I started looking for very simple patterns that would go together quickly yet complement the quilt front. I wanted people to look at my quilt backs, and I began encouraging other quilters to use the backing as an additional design opportunity. That was when the idea for this book began to take shape.

I consider my two-sided quilts reversible; they're perfect for the bedroom because they double your decorating potential. Just add pillows (a perfect way to use up even smaller fabric leftovers) and there you have it—a bedroom ensemble!

When you walk into just about any bedroom, the first thing you see is the bed, and, of course, whatever happens to be covering it! The bedcover is probably the most important decorating component in the room. The patterns and colors used on the large expanse of a bed define the decorating style and set the mood. As quilters, we know that a handmade quilt can be one of the most unique, original, and creative options for a bedcover. With the infinite variety and choices of wonderful fabrics, patterns, and techniques, it's easy to tailor make a quilt based on favorite colors, subject matter, category of quilt, or even a favorite method such as appliqué.

The focus of this book is on helping quilters make wonderful quilts and create unique looks and styles for any bedroom. With a reversible quilt as the starting point, *Sweet Dreams* shows you how to get the most mileage out of your efforts and gives you everything you need to create a total ensemble for a room. Reversible quilts are in fact two quilts that share a common batting and are then quilted and bound together. The technique offers the quilter two sides on which to display creativity. As a decorating tool, reversible quilts offer tremendous flexibility; simply flipping the quilt over can change the entire look and feel of the room.

I've included instructions for three reversible quilts in this book, each part of a larger bedroom ensemble. Each quilt pattern is presented as a separate project to be made as one side of a two-sided quilt or to stand on its own. When I made each pair of quilts, I used compatible pattern styles and colors, providing continuity from one side to the other. Each quilt was designed to have a lighter colored and a darker colored side. The lighter side of the

quilt is a perfect complement for spring and summer when the light, airy mood energizes us. The darker side helps provide a cozy and inviting atmosphere when we want to feel snug and warm during fall and winter.

In addition to the quilts, there are pillows and pillow shams to complement each ensemble. Quilters can easily make these decorating accents; they add a lovely finishing touch to the bedroom ensemble. Carefully arranged decorator pillows help tie together furnishings, while pillow shams provide a clever hideaway for bed pillows. I've included simple instructions for creating a bed skirt, so quilters will have all the information they need to stitch up the bedroom ensemble of their dreams.

Once the quilt top is complete, you'll need to decide how it will be quilted and whether it needs to be marked before layering it with batting and the backing. You'll also need to choose the batting. For machine quilting, cotton batting works best; it holds the fabric and helps to eliminate slipping and shifting of the layers. Cotton batting also gives a flatter, more old-fashioned look, but it can be harder to hand quilt. Higher loft polyester battings give a puffier, more contemporary look, similar to that of comforters.

Words of Wisdom

Be sure to give your quilt top and quilt back a good pressing before layering and basting. Trim any threads so they won't show through the light fabrics.

Layering Single-Sided Quilts

If you have decided to back the quilt with a single fabric, trim the selvages and sew the pieces together with a ½" seam. Press the seams open. The backing should be approximately 4" larger than the quilt top.

1. Place the backing wrong side up on a large, flat, clean surface. Smooth the fabric flat.
2. Spread the batting over the backing, smoothing out any wrinkles.
3. Center the quilt top right side up on top of the batting. Make sure the quilt top is lying square to the edges of the backing and that at least 2" of batting and backing extend beyond the quilt top on all sides. Smooth the top to remove any wrinkles.

See "Basting" on page 7.

Layering Two-Sided or Reversible Quilts

When finishing a two-sided quilt there are a few points to keep in mind. First, you will want to center each quilt on the other so that the borders match up. If the two designs were based on the same block size, then the quilt blocks and the borders should line up exactly. If the quilts were made up of blocks based on different sizes or there is an overall design with no specific geometric shape, then you will center one quilt over the other. Give the quilt tops a final pressing to eliminate any wrinkles and make sure the seams are flat. Follow these steps for centering and lining up the quilts.

1. Lay one of the quilts wrong side up on a large, flat, clean surface. Smooth the quilt flat. Tape the sides to the surface with masking tape. With a piece of sewing chalk, mark the center of the quilt both vertically and horizontally from top to bottom and side to side.

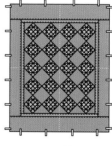 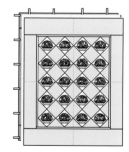

Wrong Side Up
Mark center lines
with chalk.

Right Side Up
Align chalk lines of first quilt,
batting, and second quilt.

2. Spread the batting over the backing, smoothing out any wrinkles.
3. Mark the horizontal and vertical centers of the second quilt top with chalk or pins. Lay the second quilt right side up on top of the batting. Match the quilt's vertical and horizontal centers with the bottom quilt. Smooth the top quilt so there are no wrinkles.

Basting

Two popular ways of basting are with a needle and thread and with safety pins. Thread basting is generally used when hand quilting; safety pins are usually preferred for machine quilting so that the machine does not get caught on the threads. Whichever way you choose, start at the center of the quilt and work your way diagonally to the quilt edges. Return to the center of the quilt and continue basting or pinning toward the edges to create a horizontal and then vertical grid. Finish by basting around the quilt top edges. If at any time you find wrinkles or puckers, you will need to readjust the basting so that the entire quilt will lie smooth and flat in the end.

Words of Wisdom

When basting a two-sided quilt, look at the back occasionally to see how the quilts are lining up and make any necessary adjustments.

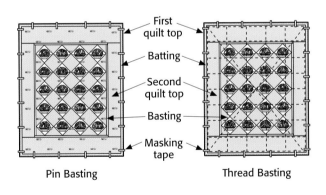

Pin Basting — First quilt top, Batting, Second quilt top, Basting, Masking tape — Thread Basting

Quilting

Quilts can be quilted by hand, by sewing machine, or by a professional machine quilter. I have found each of these quilting methods is successful when the quilt is satisfactorily basted. The decision whether to hand or machine quilt is entirely a personal one. Whichever method you choose should complement your work and ultimately bind the quilt front to the quilt back sufficiently for the type of wear you expect the quilt to be subject to.

Words of Wisdom

When making the decision whether to hand or machine quilt, remember that there will be many more seams to quilt through when quilting a reversible quilt.

Take special care when choosing quilting designs and thread color for a reversible quilt since they will show on both sides. Usually an overall quilt pattern and a neutral thread color work best. If one side of the quilt is dominant over the other, then focus special attention on that side when quilting. Just be sure to keep in mind what effect the quilting will have on the less dominant side.

A Special Note about Two-Sided Quilts and Professional Machine Quilting

Professional machine quilting is fast becoming a preferred option for many folks. You simply deliver the quilt top, batting, and backing to the machine quilter, and she or he does all the work for you. No basting is required. The quilt is pinned to the machine and stretched during the quilting process.

A word of caution for two-sided quilts: During the process of professional machine quilting, the backing material tends to stretch lengthwise, so when the quilting is finished you may have several inches of fabric extending from your quilt. Since two-sided quilts are pieced on both sides, they naturally have a lot of give to them. During professional machine quilting, the net effect can be exacerbated for two-sided quilts. That is why I always baste my two-sided quilts, even when they are to be professionally machine quilted. Discuss options in advance with a professional quilter for additional guidance.

Binding

I use a French or double-fold binding for two-sided quilts since the appearance of the binding is important on both sides. Before attaching the binding, square the quilt by trimming any uneven edges and corners. A walking foot is very helpful when sewing the binding to the quilt. It helps to feed the layers through the machine evenly.

1. Join the binding strips on the diagonal to make 1 continuous strip.

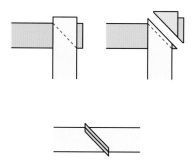

2. Cut 1 end at a 45° angle. Fold ¼" of the angled edge to the wrong side. Press the fold flat. Iron the entire binding strip in half lengthwise, wrong sides together.

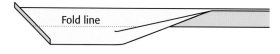

3. Align the raw edges of the binding with the raw edges of the quilt top in the middle of one side of the quilt. Begin sewing the binding 1" to 2" from the start of the binding using a ¼" seam allowance. Stop stitching ¼" from the corner of the quilt and backstitch.

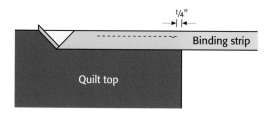

4. Remove the quilt from the machine. Fold the binding up, away from the quilt, and then back down so that the fold is even with the edge of the quilt top. Begin stitching at the edge, backstitching to secure the seam. Repeat with the remaining corners.

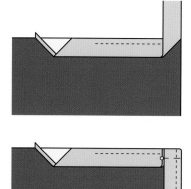

5. Join the binding ends by inserting the binding strip inside the angled end. Stitch across the remainder of the binding.

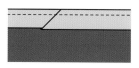

6. Roll the binding over the raw edges of the quilt to the back, just covering the machine stitching. Sew the binding in place by hand with a blind-stitch. At each corner, fold the binding as shown to form a mitered corner on both the front and the back of the quilt. Blind stitch the mitered corners.

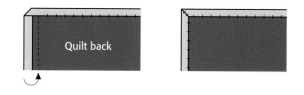

Making a Bed Skirt

Bed skirts, also called dust ruffles, complete the bedroom ensemble by concealing the box springs and bed frame. The fabric choice serves as a backdrop for the pattern and color of the quilt. It can be subtle, or more colorful to coordinate with the quilt. A bed skirt consists of two main parts: the deck, which is the large, flat piece of fabric that fits between the mattress and the box spring, and the skirt, which is attached to the deck and hangs in gathers to the floor.

Deck Preparation

Decks can be made in two ways—with a fitted sheet or by piecing yardage together as you would for a quilt backing.

To prepare a fitted sheet:
1. Purchase a fitted sheet sized for your bed.
2. Cover the box spring with the sheet and, using a fabric marking pen, draw a line along the top edge of the box spring. This line will be the seam line for attaching the skirt to the deck.

To prepare yardage lengths:
1. Measure the box spring width. Add 1" for the seam allowances.
2. Cut 2 pieces of 42"-wide fabric to this length.
3. Sew the 2 fabric pieces together along the trimmed selvages using a ½" seam allowance.
4. Measure the length of the box spring (from the head to the foot). Add 1" for the seam allowances.
5. Cut the fabric to this length.

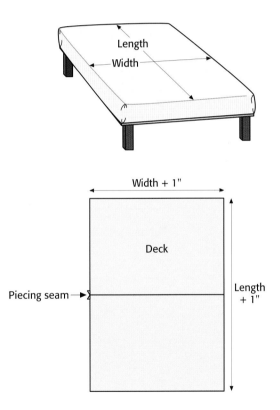

Calculating Yardage and Cutting Dimensions for the Skirt

1. Bed skirt side length (the distance from the head of the bed to the foot of the bed) equals the box spring length x 2½.

   Bed skirt side length: Box spring length _____ x 2½ = _____

2. Bed skirt width equals the box spring width x 2½.

   Bed skirt width: Box spring width _____ x 2½ = _____

3. Add the bed skirt side length and the bed skirt width together. Multiply this number by 2.

   Bed skirt side length + bed skirt width = _____ x 2 = _____

4. Divide this number by the width of the fabric you will be using (use 40" for standard quilting fabric to compensate for shrinkage and removing selvages). This number equals the number of strips you will need to cut.

   Total length = _____ divided by 40 = _____ no. of strips to cut

5. Multiply the number of strips you need to cut by the skirt drop (the distance from the top of the box spring to the floor plus 2"); divide that by 36 to convert inches to yards. This is the amount of yardage required for the bed skirt ruffle.

   No. strips to cut x [skirt drop +2] = _____ divided by 36 = _____ no. yards needed

6. The skirt drop plus 2" measurement calculated in step 5 is your strip width. Cut the fabric into the correct number of strips of that width.

Shortcut

To save time and fabric, you can eliminate one side of the bed skirt if it's not needed behind the headboard of your bed. To do the math, in step 3 of the calculations, add two lengths and one width; then move on to step 4.

Skirt Preparation

1. Calculate and cut the number of strips needed referring to "Calculating Yardage and Cutting Dimensions for the Skirt" on page 10. Sew the strips together using ½" seam allowances to form 1 long strip.
2. Cut the strips into 2 bed skirt side lengths and 2 bed skirt widths.
3. Finish the side edges using a ¼" double-fold hem.
4. Finish the bottom edges using a 1" double fold hem.
5. Machine gather the top edges. Stitch 2 rows of basting, 1 row at ⅜" seam allowance and the second at ⅝" seam allowance.

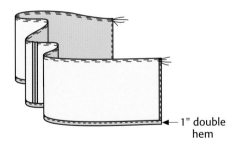

1" double hem

6. With right sides together, pin 1 bed skirt side length to the deck side edge or to the side of the fitted sheet. Adjust the gathers so they are evenly distributed.

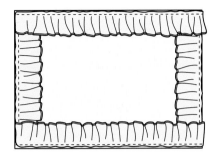

Attach each skirt section separately to deck.

7. Sew the gathers to the deck using a ½" seam allowance.
8. Repeat steps 5 and 6 for the 3 remaining sides. Press the seam allowances toward the deck and top stitch through all the layers.

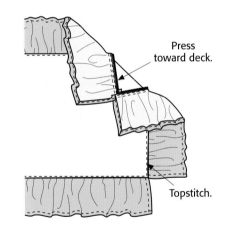

Press toward deck.

Topstitch.

Just for Fun

Piece together strips of coordinating fabrics for the ruffles of your bed skirt.

Stars Ensemble

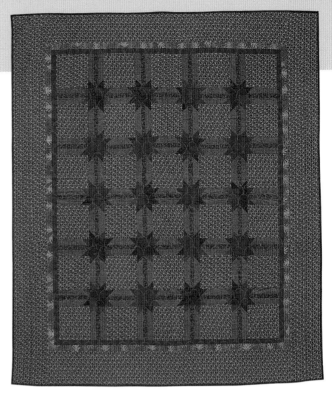

Nova

Star Quadrant

Quilts by Pamela Lindquist, 84½" x 96½".
Machine quilted by Kris Bizzarri.

A nova is a star that suddenly increases in brightness and then returns to its original appearance in several months or years. This quilt is made up of two traditional blocks, a variation of 54-40 or Fight and the Churn Dash. By alternating the placement of the blocks and using contrasting fabrics, you can almost see the stars becoming brighter and then returning to their original form. To create a reversible quilt, I paired this with the "Star Quadrant" quilt, shown above right. Instructions for the "Nova" quilt begin on page 14. If you want to make the coordinating decorator pillows, see page 22 for yardage requirements. My inspiration for "Nova" was a design in the book Make Any Block Any Size *by Joen Wolfrom.*

This simple design combined with a creative choice of color and fabric makes an attractive quilt front or back. It would be perfect for showcasing a favorite fabric in the center squares and border. The easy construction guarantees that it will go together fast. I call it "Star Quadrant" because the geometric design creates a grid that seems to align the stars. I used this as the back of "Nova," shown above left. This quilt top will be slightly larger than "Nova" (86" x 99"); it will be trimmed after quilting to match the size of "Nova." Instructions for the "Star Quadrant" quilt begin on page 19. If you want to make the coordinating pillow shams, see page 25 for additional yardage requirements.

"Nova" Quilt

Materials and Cutting

Yardage is based on 42"-wide fabric; strips are cut 42" long unless otherwise stated.

Fabric	Color and Value	Yardage	Strip Width	No. to Cut	Crosscut from Strips	Size
BLOCK 1						
Fabric A Corner four-patch unit	Medium brown prints	¾ yd. total	2½"	8	–	–
Fabric B Corner four-patch unit	Off-white prints	1⅝ yds. total	2½"	8	–	–
Star point background			2¾"	9	–	–
Fabric C Center four-patch unit	Dark red prints	1¼ yds. total	2½"	4	–	–
Star points			2¾"	9	–	–
BLOCK 2						
Fabric B Block corner background	Off-white prints	2⅜ yds. total	5½"	5	30 squares	5½" x 5½" ◻
Side four-patch units			2½"	16	–	–
Fabric C Center four-patch units	Dark red prints	⅜ yd. total	2½"	4	–	–
Fabric D Block corner triangle units	Medium pink prints	1 yd. total	5½"	5	30 squares	5½" x 5½" ◻
Inner Border 1	Medium pink print	⅜ yd.	1½"	7	–	–
Inner Border 2	Dark red print	½ yd.	1¾"	7	–	–
Inner Border 3	Medium pink print	⅝ yd.	2¼"	8	–	–
Outer Border	Dark red print	2⅜ yds.	8½"	9	–	–
Backing*	Dark print	7½ yds.	–	–	–	–
Binding	Dark print	⅝ yd.	2"	10	–	–
Batting		88" x 100" piece	–	–	–	–

* Backing fabric needed for non-reversible quilt only.

◻ *Cut squares once diagonally*

Quilt size: 84" x 96"
Block 1 finished size: 12" x 12"
Block 2 finished size: 12" x 12"

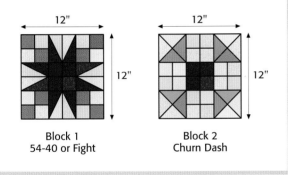

Block 1
54-40 or Fight

Block 2
Churn Dash

Shortcut

You can simplify this pattern by eliminating some of the piecing. In block 1, simply cut 4½" squares for the center units.

In block 2, substitute 4½" squares for the center units, and side center units. For the corner units, make half-square triangles. Cut 5" squares in half on the diagonal, piece them together, and trim to 4½" square.

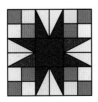

Shortcut Block 1

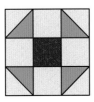

Shortcut Block 2

Making Block 1

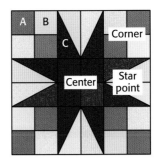

1. **Corner four-patch units:** Sew together the 2½"-wide strips of assorted fabrics A and B in pairs to make 8 strip sets. Press the seam allowances toward the darker color.

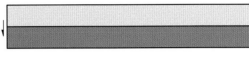

Make 8.

2. Cut the strip sets into 120 segments, each 2½" wide.

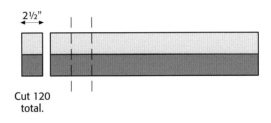

Cut 120 total.

3. Sew the segments together to make 60 four-patch corner units measuring 4½" square. Press seams open.

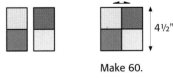

Make 60.

4. **Center four-patch unit:** Using the 2½"-wide fabric C strips, repeat steps 1 through 3 above to make 2 strip sets. Cut thirty 2½" units from the strip sets to make 15 Four Patch blocks.

Make 15.

5. **Star-point units:** Lay two 2¾"-wide strips of fabric B wrong sides together. Cut the strips into 5¼" segments to create a total of sixty 2¾" x 5¼" rectangles. Keep the rectangles wrong sides together for the next step.

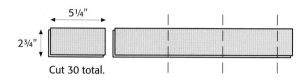

Cut 30 total.

6. Cut each rectangle in half diagonally to make 2 pairs of triangles that are mirror images. Make a template using the pattern below. Use the template to mark the dots and trim the point on each triangle.

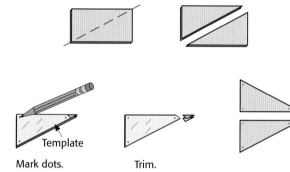

Mark dots.   Trim.

7. Repeat steps 5 and 6 using the dark print C fabrics.

8. Sew the fabric B and fabric C triangles together along the diagonal edge. Pin if necessary and be sure to match the dots. Press the seam allowances toward the darker fabric.

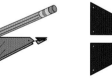

Make 60.   Make 60.

9. Sew the mirror-image triangle units together to make 60 star-point units.

Make 60.

10. Arrange the corner units, center unit, and star-point units as shown. Sew the units together in rows. Press the seam allowances in opposite directions from row to row. Sew the rows together. Press the seam allowances in one direction. Make 15.

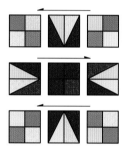 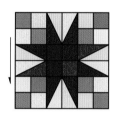

Block 1
Make 15.

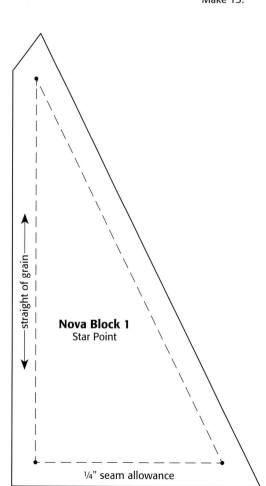

straight of grain

Nova Block 1
Star Point

¼" seam allowance

Making Block 2

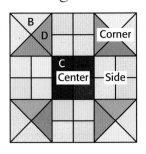

1. **Corner units:** Mix and match the fabric B half-square triangles. Sew along the diagonal. Press the seam allowance open. Cut the square on the opposite diagonal through the seam to create 60 side-by-side triangle units.

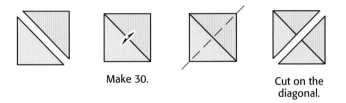

Make 30.

Cut on the diagonal.

2. Repeat for the fabric D half-square triangles.

3. Join the fabric B and fabric D triangle units together. Sew along the diagonal, matching the center seams. Press seam allowances toward darker color. Use a square ruler and trim the corner unit to measure exactly 4½" square. Align the 45° angle of the ruler with the diagonal seam line and trim all 4 sides; keep the center of the block centered at the point on the ruler where 2¼" intersects the 45° angle line. The original squares were cut slightly oversized to allow for this final squaring up.

Make 60.

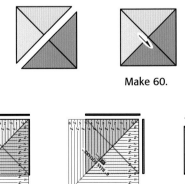

Trim first two sides.

Trim last two sides.

4½"

4½"

Corner Unit
Make 60.

4. **Center and side four-patch units:** Follow steps 1 through 3 for block 1 on page 15; sew together 2½"-wide strips of assorted fabric B to make 8 strip sets. Make 60 side four-patch units. Repeat, using 2½"-wide strips of fabric C to make 2 strip sets. Cut thirty 2½" segments and make 15 four-patch units for the center.

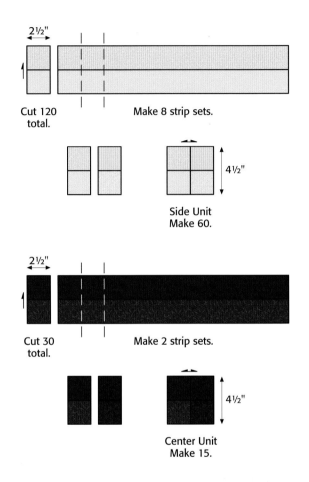

2½"

Cut 120 total.

Make 8 strip sets.

4½"

Side Unit
Make 60.

2½"

Cut 30 total.

Make 2 strip sets.

4½"

Center Unit
Make 15.

5. Arrange the corner units and four-patch units as shown. Sew the units together in rows. Press the seam allowances in opposite directions from row to row. Sew the rows together. Press the seam allowances in one direction. Make 15.

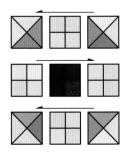

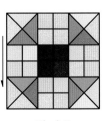

Block 2
Make 15.

Quilt Top Assembly

1. Arrange blocks 1 and 2 as shown in the quilt diagram.
2. Sew the blocks together in rows. Press the seam allowances in opposite directions from row to row.
3. Sew the rows together. Press the seam allowances in the same direction.

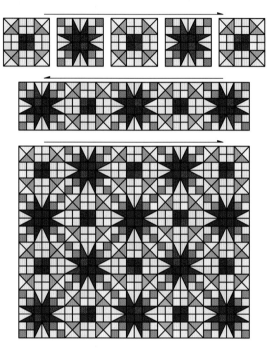

Borders

1. Join the strips for the first inner border from end to end to make 1 continuous strip of fabric.
2. Measure the length of the quilt top through the center. From the continuous strip, cut 2 borders to that length. Pin and sew the borders to the sides of the quilt top. Press the seam allowances toward the borders.
3. Measure the width of the quilt top through the center. From the continuous strip, cut 2 borders to that length. Pin and sew the borders to the top and bottom of the quilt top. Press the seam allowances toward the borders.
4. Repeat steps 1 through 3 for the 3 remaining border fabrics.

Quilt Finishing

To complete the quilt, see "Finishing Your Quilt" on pages 6–8.

"Star Quadrant" Quilt

Materials and Cutting

Yardage is based on 42"-wide fabric; all strips are cut 42" long unless otherwise stated.

Fabric	Color and Value	Yardage	Strip Width	No. to Cut	Crosscut from Strips	Size
Fabric A Center sashing strip	Dark brown print	⅞ yd.	2"	13	–	–
Fabric B Outer sashing strips	Medium brown print	1⅝ yds.	2"	26	–	–
Fabric C Star points	Medium to dark red prints	1½ yd.	2¾"	12	160 squares	2¾" x 2¾"
Star center			5"	3	20 squares	5" x 5"
Fabric D* Unpieced squares	Medium red print	2¼ yds.	9"	8	30 squares	9" x 9"
Inner Border	Dark red print	½ yd.	1½"	8	–	–
Middle Border	Medium red print	⅝ yd.	2"	8	–	–
Outer Border*	Medium red print	3¼ yds.	10½"	10	–	–
Backing**	Dark print	7½ yds.	–	–	–	–
Binding	Dark red print	⅝ yd.	2"	10	–	–
Batting		88" x 100" piece	–	–	–	–

**If you want the unpieced squares and outer-border fabric to match, you will need 5½ yards total.*

***Backing fabric needed for non-reversible quilt only.*

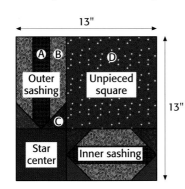

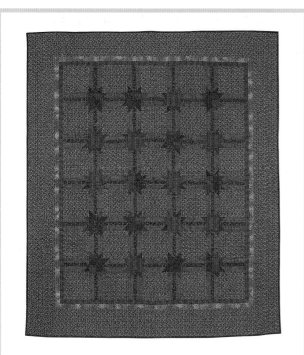

Quilt size: 84" x 96"
Finished block size: 13" x 13"

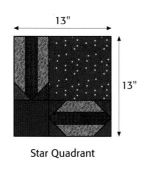

Star Quadrant

Piecing the Quilt Top

1. **Sashing units:** Sew 2"-wide strips of fabric B to both sides of a 2"-wide strip of fabric A to make 13 strip sets. Press the seam allowances toward the darker fabric.

Make 13.

2. Cut the strip sets into 9"-wide segments to create 49 rectangles.

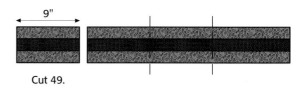

Cut 49.

3. Place a 2¾" fabric C square in one corner of a sashing rectangle right sides together. Stitch across the diagonal. Trim the corners, leaving a ¼" seam allowance. Press the corner square open.

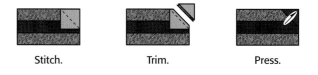

Stitch.   Trim.   Press.

4. Place a second 2¾" square on the adjacent corner of the rectangle. Stitch across the diagonal. Trim and press as before. Repeat steps 3 through 5 on all 49 sashing rectangles.

Make 49.

5. Stitch two 2¾" squares to the remaining corners of 31 of the sashing rectangles. Trim and press as described in step 5.

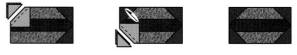

Make 31.

Just for Fun

To add variety to the quilt and use up scraps, piece some random four-patch units in place of the 5" squares that create the center of the stars. Cut four 2¾" squares from scrap fabrics and sew them together to make the four-patch unit.

---

7. Arrange the inner sashing units, outer sashing units, 9" squares, and 5" squares in rows as shown in the quilt layout.

8. Sew the units together to create rows. Press the seam allowances toward the unpieced squares in each row.

9. Sew the rows together. Press the seam allowances in one direction.

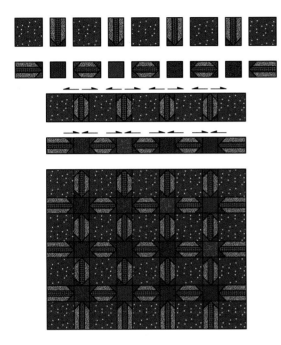

Borders

1. Join the strips for the first border end to end to make 1 long continuous strip of fabric.

2. Measure the length of the quilt top through the center. From the continuous strip, cut 2 borders to that length. Pin and sew the borders to the sides of the quilt top. Press the seam allowances toward the border.

3. Measure the width of the quilt top through the center. From the continuous strip, cut 2 borders to that length. Pin and sew the borders to the top and bottom of the quilt top. Press the seam allowances toward the borders.

4. Repeat steps 1 through 3 for the 2 remaining border fabrics.

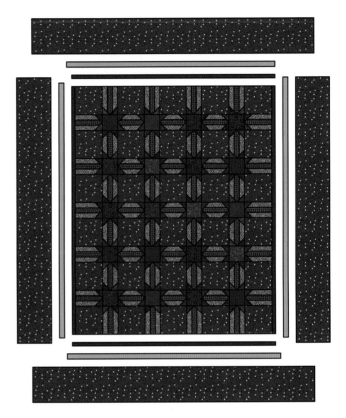

Quilt Finishing

To complete the quilt, see "Finishing Your Quilt" on pages 6–8.

"Nova" Decorator Pillows

Materials and Cutting for 2 Pillows

Yardage is based on 42"-wide fabric; strips are cut 42" long unless otherwise stated.

Fabric	Color and Value	Yardage	Strip Width	No. to Cut	Crosscut from Strips	Size
Fabric A Corner four-patch unit	Medium brown print	⅛ yd.	2½"	1	–	–
Fabric B Corner four-patch unit	3 off-white prints	⅛ yd. each	2½"	1	–	–
Star-point background			2¾"	2 (1 strip from each)	8 (4 from each strip)	2¾" x 5¼"
Fabric C Center four-patch unit	4 dark red prints	⅛ yd. each	2½"	2 (1 strip from each)	–	–
Star points			2¾"	2 (1 strip from each)	8 (4 from each strip)	2¾" x 5¼"
Inner Border	Medium red print	⅜ yd.	2½"	4	4 strips 4 strips	2½" x 12½" 2½" x 16½"
Outer Border	Dark red print	⅜ yd.	2½"	4	4 strips 4 strips	2½" x 16½" 2½" x 20½"
Scrap Backing		Two 18" x 18" pieces	–	–	–	–
Backing		1⅜ yds.	–	–	2 rectangles 2 rectangles	15½" x 20½" 12" x 20½"
Batting		Two 18" x 18" pieces	–	–	–	–
Fusible Interfacing (optional)		⅝ yd.	–	–	–	–
Two Pillow Forms		16" x 16"	–	–	–	–

Designed to be companions for the "Nova" quilt on page 15, these pillows go together quickly. Use the same fabrics as for the quilt, or add some fabrics from your stash as well.

Finished size: 20" x 20"
Fits a standard 16" x 16" pillow form

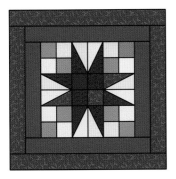

54-40 or Fight

Pillow Front Assembly
(Instructions for 1 Pillow)

1. Follow the instructions below and on pages 15–16 to construct block 1 from the "Nova" quilt pattern.
   Corner four-patch unit: Make 1 strip set; cut 8 segments to make 4 units.
   Center four-patch unit: Make 1 strip set; cut 2 segments to make 1 unit.
   Star point unit: Make 4 units.

2. Pin and sew a 2½" x 12½" strip of the inner-border fabric to each side of the block. Press the seam allowances toward the border. Pin and sew the 2½" x 16½" inner-border strips to the top and bottom of the block. Press the seam allowances toward the border.

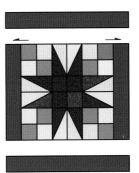

Make 1.

Just for Fun

Make two of the Churn Dash blocks (block 2 from "Nova") in place of the Star blocks and follow the instructions here to make a variation on these decorator pillows.

3. Layer the bordered block with an 18" square of batting and an 18" square of scrap backing. Baste the layers together.
4. Quilt the block in the same quilting design as used for the "Nova" quilt, or choose a pattern that enhances the star. Trim the excess batting and backing even with the edges of the bordered block.

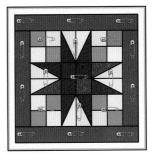

5. The outer-border strips will create the flange of the finished pillow. Apply fusible interfacing to the 2½"-wide outer-border strips to stiffen them slightly and add body, if desired. Stitch the outer-border strips to the pillow front.

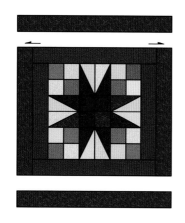

Pillow Back Assembly

1. Sew a 1" double-fold hem on a 20½" side of each piece of the pillow backing fabric. First fold the raw edge over 1" to the wrong side and press. Fold and press again; then stitch close to the edge as shown.

First fold   Fold again and stitch.

2. With right sides together, center the hemmed edge of the shorter pillow back onto the pillow front and align the raw edges. Pin and sew around the outer edges using a ¼" seam allowance.

3. With right sides together overlap the second piece of the backing fabric 3" from the center-line. Align the raw edges and pin in place. Sew the outer edges using a ¼" seam allowance.

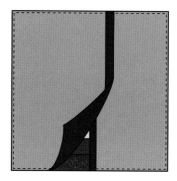

4. Turn the pillow right side out. Press.
5. With the pillow top facing up, stitch along the seam between the two borders to create a 2" flange around the pillow form. Insert the pillow form into the pillow.

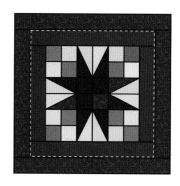

Shortcut

It's not necessary to slipstitch the pillow opening closed; the overlap will keep the pillow form secure. Then you can easily pop the pillow form out and use it in another pillow whenever the mood strikes you.

"Star Quadrant" Pillow Shams

Materials and Cutting for 2 Pillow Shams

Yardage is based on 42"-wide fabric; strips are cut 42" long unless otherwise stated.

Fabric	Color and Value	Yardage	Strip Width	No. to Cut	Crosscut from Strips	Size
Fabric A						
Center sashing strip	Dark brown print	⅜ yd.	2"	4	4 strips	2" x 19½"
					4 strips	2" x 11½"
Fabric B						
Outer sashing strips	Medium brown print	⅝ yd.	2"	8	8 strips	2" x 19½"
					8 strips	2" x 11½"
Fabric C*						
Star points	Medium to dark red prints	¾ yd. total	2¾"	5	64 squares	2¾" x 2¾"
Star center			5"	1	8 squares	5" x 5"
Fabric D						
Pillow center and outer border	Medium red print	1⅛ yd.	11½"	1	2 rectangles	11½" x 19½"
			3½"	7	4 strips	3½" x 19½"
			–	–	4 strips	3½" x 11½"
			–	–	16 rectangles	3½" x 5"
			–	–	8 squares	3½" x 3½"
Scrap Backing		Two 22" x 30" pieces	–	–	–	–
Backing	Medium red print	2⅜ yd.	26½"	1	2 rectangles	19¼" x 26½"
			24¼"	2	2 rectangles	24¼" x 26½"
Batting		Two 22" x 30" pieces	–	–	–	–
Fusible Interfacing (optional)		1½ yds.	–	–	–	–

* *If you want to make the star points scrappy, cut your 2¾" squares from several different red prints.*

These striking pillow shams are companions for the "Star Quadrant" quilt on page 20. Use the same fabrics as used in the quilt, or incorporate other scraps and coordinating fabrics from your stash.

Finished size: 26" x 34"
Fits a standard 20" x 26" bed pillow

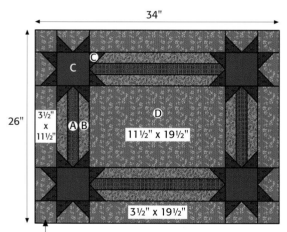

Note: Interior dimensions are unfinished, cut sizes.

Pillow Sham Front Assembly
(Instructions for 1 Sham)

1. Make 2 sashing units by sewing the 11½" strips of fabrics A and B together as illustrated on page 20. Repeat to make 2 sashing units of the 19½" strips of fabrics A and B.

2. Follow steps 3 through 5 on page 20 to sew a fabric C square to each corner of all the sashing units.

3. Arrange the units as shown to create the sham and sew them together in rows. Press the seam allowances toward the fabric C squares in the top and bottom rows. Press toward fabric D in the center row. Sew the rows together. Press the seam allowances in one direction.

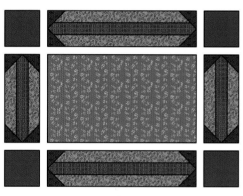

Make 1.

4. Layer the step 3 unit with a 22" x 30" piece of batting and a 22"x 30" piece of scrap fabric to be used as a backing. Baste the layers together.

5. Quilt the block in the same pattern you used on the "Star Quadrant" quilt or choose a pattern that enhances the star portion in the corners. Trim the excess batting and backing even with the outside edges of the block.

6. Sew 2 fabric C squares to the corners of eight 3½" x 5" pieces of fabric D. Stitch along the diagonal and trim the seam allowances to ¼".

Make 8.

7. Piece the outer-border strips together with the step 6 units and the 3½" fabric D squares as shown to create side, top, and bottom flanges. If desired, use fusible interfacing to stiffen the borders and add extra body to the flanges. Sew the borders to the main section of the pillow beginning with the sides.

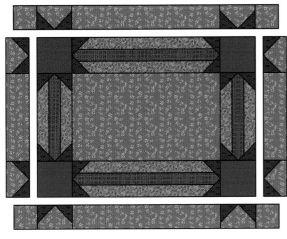

Make 1.

Pillow Sham Back Assembly

1. Sew a 1" double-fold hem on one 26½" side of 2 backing pieces. First fold the raw edge over 1" to the wrong side and press. Fold over 1" and press again; then stitch the hem close to the edge.

2. With right sides together, center the hemmed edge of the 17¼" x 26½" pillow back onto the pillow front. Align the raw edges and pin in place. Sew around the outer edges using a ¼" seam allowance.

3. With right sides together, overlap the second piece of backing fabric 5" from the centerline. Align the raw edges and pin in place. Sew the outer edges together using a ¼" seam allowance.

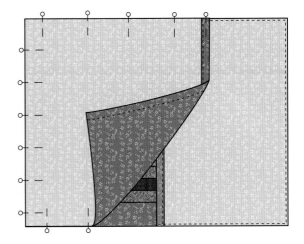

4. Turn the sham right side out. Press.
5. From the pillow sham front, stitch along the inside border seam to create a 3" flange around the edges. Insert a pillow.

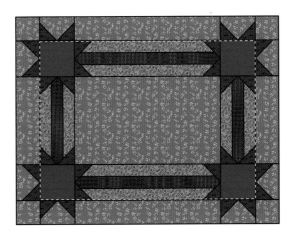

Floral Baskets Ensemble

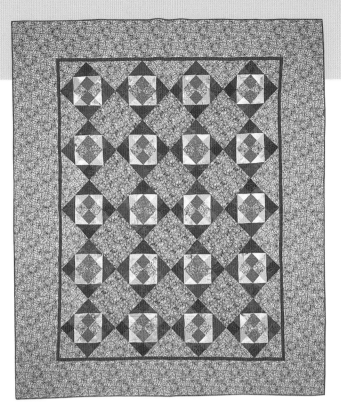

Blooming Baskets

Stepping Stones

Quilts by Pamela Lindquist, 94½" x 111½".
Machine quilted by Kris Bizzarri.

These simple country baskets are filled with fantasy flowers in all shades of blue to create a spring fling any time of the year. If you prefer, use a multitude of colors. This quilt was designed to be the quilt top for the "Blooming Baskets" quilt ensemble; the "Stepping Stones" quilt, shown above right, was designed as the back. Instructions for the "Blooming Baskets" quilt begin on page 30. If you want to make the coordinating decorator pillows, see page 38 for yardage requirements.

I often include a small surpise element in my quilts. In "Blooming Baskets," I replaced a flower with a bird in just one of the baskets. Feel free to add a nesting bird to as many flower baskets as you like.

This square within a square—or diamond within a diamond—block requires fabrics of different values to create the geometric pattern similar to the facets of a diamond gemstone. The pieced blocks are placed between floral squares to give the impression of stepping stones in a garden. This quilt was designed to be the quilt back for "Blooming Baskets," but it could stand on its own as a striking but simple quilt top. Instructions for the "Stepping Stones" quilt begin on page 35. If you want to make the coordinating ruffled pillow shams, see page 41 for yardage requirements.

"Blooming Baskets" Quilt

Materials and Cutting

Yardage is based on 42"-wide fabric; all strips are cut 42" long unless otherwise stated.

Fabric	Color and Value	Yardage	Strip Width	No. to Cut	Crosscut from Strips	Size
Fabric A Basket block background	Light solid or subtle print	3⅝ yds.	14½"	6	10 squares 10 squares*	14½" x 14½" ◹ 6¾" x 6¾" ◹
			2¼"	14	40 strips	2¼" x 11¼"
Fabric B Basket	Medium tan print	1⅝ yds.**	9"	3	10 squares	9" x 9" ◹
			1½" bias strips	Approx. 360" total	–	–
Fabric C Basket accent	Dark brown print	⅝ yd.	1½" bias strips	Approx. 250" total	–	–
Fabric D Flowers and bird	Medium to dark blue prints	⅞ yd. total	–	–	100 flowers	Template patterns on pages 33–34.
Fabric E Leaves	Medium to dark green prints	¾ yd. total	–	–	140 leaves	Template pattern on page 34.
Fabric F Piping	Medium to dark green	¾ yds.	¾"	27	80 strips	¾" x 12½"
Fabric G Alternate blocks, side and corner triangles	Medium blue print	3 yds.	18¼" 12½" 9½"	2 4 1	4 squares 12 squares 2 squares	18¼" x 18¼" ⊠ 12½" x 12½" 9½" x 9½" ◹
Inner Border	Dark green print	½ yd.	1½"	8	–	–
Outer Border	Medium blue print	3⅞ yds.	12½"	10	–	–
Backing***		8½ yds.	–	–	–	–
Binding	Medium or dark blue print	¾ yd.	2"	11	–	–
Batting		98" x 115" piece	–	–	–	–
Fusible Web (optional)		3 yds, 17" wide	–	–	–	–

* Cut these squares from the leftover 14½" strips.

** Cut the three 9" strips first. Reserve the rest for cutting bias strips for the basket handles.

*** Backing fabric needed for non-reversible quilt only.

◹ Cut squares once diagonally

⊠ Cut squares twice diagonally

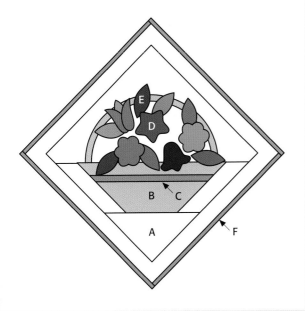

Quilt size: 94" x 111"
Finished block size: 12" x 12"

Cutting the Bias Strips

1. Cut the remaining fabric B and the entire ⅝ yard of fabric C into 1½" wide bias strips for the basket handles and accent strips. To cut bias strips, use a clear plastic ruler and a rotary cutter to cut the fabric selvage to selvage at a 45° angle as shown. Use the cut edge to measure and cut the 1½"-wide strips.

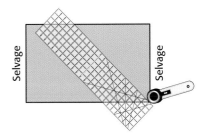

2. Sew the fabric B strips together to make 1 continuous strip. Fold in half lengthwise with wrong sides together and press. Cut into twenty 18" lengths for the basket handles. Repeat for fabric C. Cut the folded fabric C bias strips into twenty 12" lengths.

Basket Handles

1. Make a template for placement of the basket handle using the pattern on page 34. Lightly trace the curve onto the fabric A background triangle (cut from the 14½" squares) using a pencil or fabric marker. Fold the background triangle in half to mark the center point if desired. Align it with the center of the curve.

2. Place the raw edges of the folded basket-handle bias strip just inside and below the placement line. Sew the strip to the background triangle by machine or by hand using a scant ¼" seam allowance.

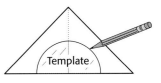

3. Roll the folded edge over the raw edge of the bias strip, and hand sew the folded edge of the basket handle bias strip to the background fabric.

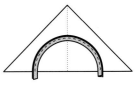

4. Trim the ends of the bias strip that extend beyond the edge of the block. Repeat to make 20 basket handles for the blocks.

Basket Accent Strip

1. Lay the raw edges of the bias strip 1½" from the long side of the basket fabric triangle. Sew it to the basket triangle by machine, stitching ¼" from the raw edges.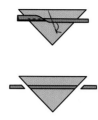

2. Roll the folded edge of the strip over the raw edges toward the bottom of the basket. Hand sew the strip to the background. Trim the bias that extends beyond the edges. Make 20.

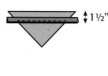

Make 20.

Assembling the Basket Block

1. Pin a 2¼" x 11¼" fabric A strip to each side of the basket triangle as shown. Sew, and press the seam allowances toward the basket.

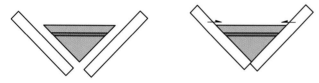

2. Trim the fabric A pieces across the basket top so there is a straight line across the top.

3. Measure 4½" from the basket top and trim the extra fabric from the basket bottom.

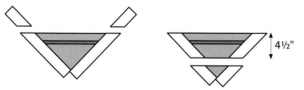

4. Assemble the basket handles, basket bottoms, and fabric A background triangles as shown. Stitch together to make 20 blocks. Do not trim the block edges until the appliqué is complete. Some distortion may occur with appliqué; waiting to

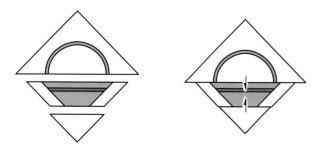

cut the blocks until the appliqué is finished will help guarantee that your blocks will measure 12½" square.

Appliquéing the Flowers and Leaves

1. Choose your favorite appliqué method: hand, machine, or fusible. Make templates for the flowers and leaf using the patterns on pages 33–34. Add a scant ¼" seam allowance to each flower and leaf shape if you will be turning under the edges of your appliqué shapes.

2. Cut 100 flowers from fabric D or from scraps.

3. Cut 140 leaves from fabric E or from scraps.

4. Use the Basket block illustration on page 31 as a guide to place the flowers and leaves in the basket. You don't need to worry about exact placement. I varied the position and colors of the flowers and leaves in each basket for more interest.

5. Appliqué the flowers and the leaves to the Basket block.

6. When the blocks are completed, trim them to 12½" square. Use a 12½" square ruler, placing the midpoint, 6¼", on the center of the block.

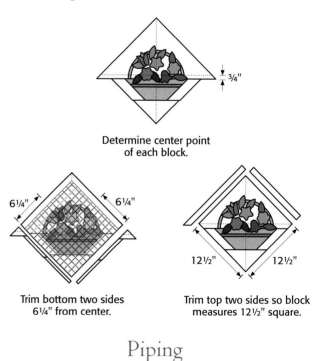

Determine center point
of each block.

Trim bottom two sides
6¼" from center.

Trim top two sides so block
measures 12½" square.

Piping

1. Fold each fabric F strip in half lengthwise with wrong sides together. Press.

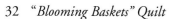

2. Sew 1 strip to each side of the Basket block in the order shown. Match the raw edges of the piping strips with the raw edges of the block and use a ⅛" seam allowance. Press flat; do not flip the piping back toward the seam allowance.

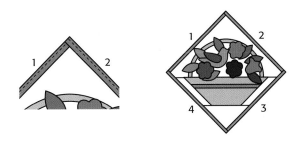

Quilt Assembly

1. Arrange the Basket blocks and the fabric G alternate blocks and side and corner triangles as shown in the assembly diagram.
2. Sew the blocks together in diagonal rows. Press the seam allowances toward the fabric G blocks and triangles.
3. Sew the rows together and press all the seam allowances in the same direction.

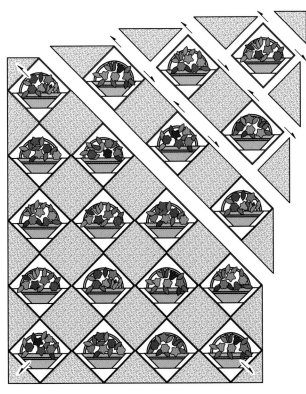

Assembly Diagram

Borders

1. Join the strips for the inner border from end to end to make 1 continuous strip of fabric.
2. Measure the length of the quilt top through the center. From the continuous strip, cut 2 borders to that length. Pin and sew the borders to the sides of the quilt top. Press the seam allowances toward the borders.
3. Measure the width of the quilt top through the center. From the continuous strip, cut 2 borders to that length. Pin and sew the borders to the top and bottom of the quilt top. Press the seam allowances toward the borders.
4. Repeat steps 1 through 3 for the outer border.

Quilt Finishing

Refer to "Finishing Your Quilt" on pages 6–8.

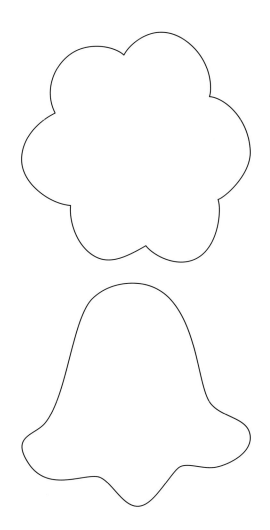

Basket Handle Placement Guide

Center of curve. Flip pattern along this line.

Place along edge of basket.

"Stepping Stones" Quilt

Materials and Cutting

Yardage is based on 42"-wide fabric; all strips are cut 42" long unless otherwise stated.

Fabric	Color and Value	Yardage	Strip Width	No. to Cut	Crosscut from Strips	Size
Fabric A Stepping Stone block	Dark blue prints	1⅞ yds. total	3½" 3⅞"	8 8	80 squares 80 squares	3½" x 3½" 3⅞" x 3⅞" ◹
Fabric B Stepping Stone block	Light blue prints	1 yd. total	3⅞"	8	80 squares	3⅞" x 3⅞" ◹
Fabric C Stepping Stone block	Dark or medium blue prints	½ yd. total	3½"	4	40 squares	3½" x 3½"
Fabric D Stepping Stone block	Medium or light blue prints	½ yd. total	3½"	4	40 squares	3½" x 3½"
Fabric E Alternate blocks	Medium blue print	1⅝ yds.	12½"	4	12 squares	12½" x 12½"
Fabric F* Side and corner setting triangles	Medium blue print	1½ yds.	18¼" 9½"	2 1	4 squares 2 squares	18¼" x 18¼" ⊠ 9½" x 9½" ◹
Inner Border	Dark blue print	½ yd.	1½"	8	–	–
Outer Border*	Medium or dark blue print	3⅞ yds.	12½"	10	–	–
Backing**		8½ yds.	–	–	–	–
Binding	Dark blue print	¾ yd.	2"	11	–	–
Batting		98" x 115" piece	–	–	–	–

* *If you want the side and corner setting triangles and the outer border to be made of the same fabric, you will need 5⅜ yards.*

** *Backing fabric needed for non-reversible quilt only.*

◹ *Cut squares diagonally once.*

⊠ *Cut squares diagonally twice.*

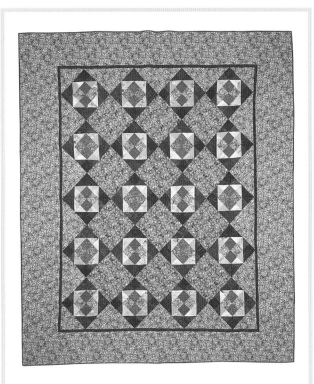

Quilt size: 94" x 111"
Finished block size: 12" x 12"

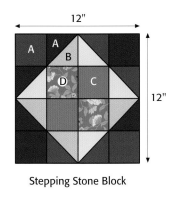

Stepping Stone Block

Words of Wisdom

The quilt shown in the photograph is done in a controlled scrappy style. The success of this quilt pattern depends largely on the use of color value to give the illusion of a diamond within a diamond. If you are using scraps, be sure to divide the colors into three distinctive groups of light, medium, and dark.

Stepping Stone Block Construction

1. Align 1 fabric A and 1 fabric B triangle, right sides together. Sew along the diagonal. Press toward the darker fabric. Repeat to make 160 half-square-triangle units measuring 3½" square.

Make 160.

2. Using the illustration below as a guide, arrange the dark, medium, and light 3½" squares and the 3½" half-square-triangle units to create the Stepping Stone block. Use the same 2 C and D fabrics in any 1 block. Sew the squares together into rows. Press the seam allowances in opposite directions from row to row. Sew the rows together. Press the seam allowances in one direction. Make 20 Stepping Stone blocks.

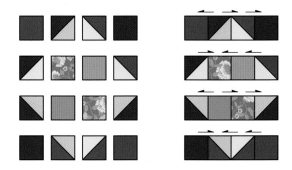

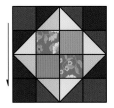

Make 20.

Quilt Top Assembly

1. Arrange the pieced blocks, fabric E alternate block squares, and fabric F side and corner setting triangles as in the assembly diagram.
2. Sew the blocks together in diagonal rows. Press the seam allowances toward the fabric E squares and fabric F triangles.
3. Sew the rows together and press all the seam allowances in the same direction.

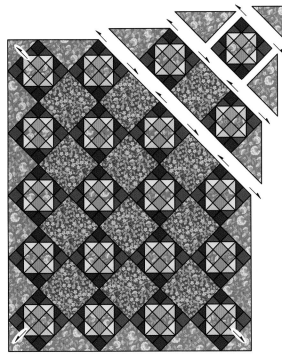

Assembly Diagram

Borders

1. Join the strips for the inner border from end to end to make 1 continuous strip of fabric.
2. Measure the length of the quilt top through the center. From the continuous strip, cut 2 borders to that length. Pin and sew the borders to the sides of the quilt top. Press the seam allowances toward the borders.
3. Measure the width of the quilt top through the center. From the continuous strip, cut 2 borders to that length. Pin and sew the borders to the top and bottom of the quilt top. Press the seam allowances toward the borders.
4. Repeat steps 1–3 for the outer border.

Quilt Finishing

Refer to "Finishing Your Quilt" on pages 6–8.

Just for Fun

Save scraps from your ensemble projects to use as accents on your curtains. Or use leftover strips for curtain tiebacks.

"Blooming Baskets" Decorator Pillows

Materials and Cutting for 2 Pillows

Yardage is based on 42"-wide fabric; cut strips 42" long unless otherwise stated.

Fabric	Color and Value	Yardage	Strip Width	No. to Cut	Crosscut from Strips	Size
Fabric A Block background	Light solid or subtle print	⅝ yd.	– – 2¼"	– – 2	1 square 1 square 4 strips	14½" x 14½" ⧅ 6¾" x 6¾" ⧅ 2¼" x 11¼"
Fabric B Basket and handle	Medium tan print	⅜ yd.	– 1½" bias strips	– Two 18" long strips	1 square –	9" x 9" ⧅ –
Fabric C Basket accent strip	Dark brown print	Scrap	1½" bias strips	Two 10" long strips	–	–
Fabric D Flowers	Medium to dark blue prints	⅛ yd. total	–	–	–	–
Fabric E Leaves	Medium green prints	⅛ yd. total	–	–	–	–
Fabric F Piping	Dark green print	⅛ yd.	¾"	3	8 strips	¾" x 12½"
Border	Medium blue print	½ yd.	2¾"	4	4 strips 4 strips	2¾" x 12½" 2¾" x 17"
Ruffle	Medium blue print	1½ yd.	6"	8	–	–
Scrap Backing		Two 18" x 18" squares	–	–	–	–
Backing	Blue print	1⅛ yd.	17"	2	2 rectangles 2 rectangles	10½" x 17" 13½" x 17"
Batting		Two 18" x 18" squares	–	–	–	–
Fusible Interfacing (optional)		2⅜ yd., 17" wide	–	–	–	–

⧅ *Cut squares once diagonally.*

These pillows are designed to be companions for the "Blooming Baskets" quilt on page 31. Use the same or similar fabrics as in the quilt, or incorporate scraps and coordinating fabrics from your stash, too.

One charming aspect of this design is that you can experiment with different flower shapes and sizes. Don't limit yourself to the patterns given. Use your imagination to create flower shapes that are unique to your quilt.

Finished size: 21" x 21"
Fits a standard 16" x 16" pillow form

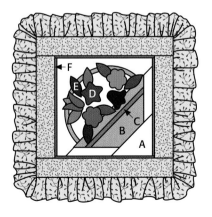

Pillow Front Assembly
(Instructions for 1 Pillow)

1. Fold 1 fabric B and 1 fabric C bias strip in half lengthwise with wrong sides together and press.
2. Follow the directions beginning with "Basket Handles" on page 31 to make a Basket block, complete with piping.
3. Pin and sew the 2¾" x 12½" border strips to the sides of the Basket block. Press the seam allowances towards the border. Pin and sew the 2¾" x 17" border strips to the block top and bottom. Press.

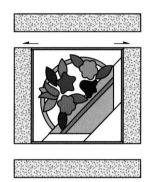

4. Layer the bordered block with an 18" x 18" piece of batting and an 18" x 18" piece of scrap backing. Baste the layers together.
5. Quilt the block using the same pattern as on the "Blooming Basket" quilt, or choose a quilting design that highlights the pieced basket.
6. Stitch around the outside of the bordered pillow block through all 3 layers using a ⅛" seam allowance. Trim the excess batting and scrap backing to match the bordered block.

Baste and trim.

Pillow Ruffle

1. Sew four 6"-wide ruffle strips end to end to create 1 continuous length. This will result in a large "tube" or "ring" of fabric. Press the seams open.
2. If you are using fusible interfacing to stiffen and add body to the ruffle, iron 3"-wide interfacing strips onto the wrong side of half of the ruffle fabric's 6" width.
3. Fold the ruffle in half wrong sides together. Press.
4. Use a basting stitch to sew ¼" inside the raw edges of the ruffle.
5. Pull the bobbin thread to create gathers until the ruffle is approximately 68" long.

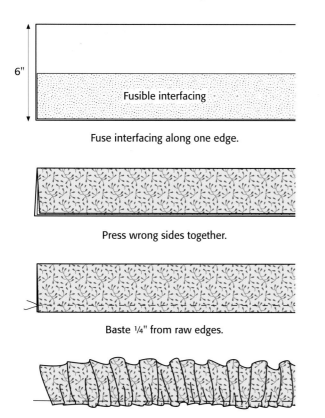

6"

Fusible interfacing

Fuse interfacing along one edge.

Press wrong sides together.

Baste ¼" from raw edges.

Gather until ruffle is approximately 68" long.

6. Pin the gathered ruffle fabric around the outside of the pillow block, distributing the gathers evenly.
7. Baste the ruffle in place with a ¼" seam allowance.

Pillow Back Assembly

1. Sew a 1" double-fold hem along the 17" edge of each backing fabric piece. To do this, fold the raw edge over 1" and press; fold over 1" again and press. Stitch close to the inner folded edge.
2. Lay a 10½" x 17" backing fabric piece with right sides together on the top of the pillow front, aligning the double-fold hem edge with the center of the pillow. Take care to tuck the ruffle in toward the center of the Basket block. Pin into place.
3. Lay the second backing on top of the first, overlapping the hemmed edge 3". Pin into place.
4. Sew the layers together along the outside edges of the Basket block using a ½" seam allowance. Turn the pillow right side out. Insert a pillow form.

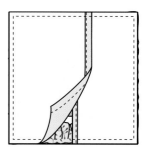

Stitch with ½" seam allowance.

"Stepping Stones" Pillow Shams

Materials and Cutting for 2 Pillow Shams

Yardage is based on 42"-wide fabric; cut all strips 42" long unless otherwise indicated.

Fabric	Color and Value	Yardage	Strip Width	No. to Cut	Crosscut from Strips	Size
Fabric A Pieced block and border	Dark blue prints	1⅛ yd. total	3⅞"	2	18 squares	3⅞" x 3⅞"
			3½"	1	8 squares	3½" x 3½"
			4¼"	4	4 strips	4¼" x 26½"
			7¾"	1	4 squares	7¾" x 7¾" ◻
Fabric B Pieced block	Light blue prints	⅜ yd. total	3⅞"	2	12 squares	3⅞" x 3⅞" ◻
Fabric C Pieced block	Medium blue print	¼ yd.	3½"	1	8 squares	3½" x 3½"
Fabric D Pieced block	Medium blue print	¼ yd.	3½"	1	8 squares	3½" x 3½"
Ruffle	Medium blue print	3 yds.	8"	12	–	–
Scrap Backing		Two 22" x 28" pieces	–	–	–	–
Backing	Blue print	1¼ yd.	21"	2	2 rectangles 2 rectangles	15½" x 21" 20½" x 21"
Batting		Two 22" x 28" pieces	–	–	–	–
Fusible Interfacing (optional)		3½ yds., 17" wide	–	–	–	–

◻ *Cut squares diagonally once.*

These pillow shams are designed to accompany the "Stepping Stones" quilt on page 36. Use the same or similar fabrics to the quilt; you may also want to incorporate other fabrics from your stash into the project if you like a scrappy look.

Finished size: 27" x 33"
Fits a standard 20" x 26" bed pillow

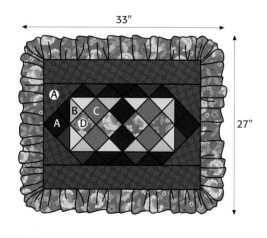

Pillow Sham Front Assembly
(Instructions for I Sham)

1. Make 6 half-square-triangle units from fabric A and B triangles.
2. Arrange the half-square-triangle units, half the 3½" squares, and half the remaining fabric A triangles as shown. Sew the units together

to form rows. Press the seam allowances in opposite directions from row to row. Sew the rows together. Press the seam allowances in one direction.

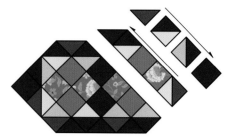

3. The fabric A corner triangles are cut slightly oversize. Sew 4 triangles to the pieced unit as shown below. Press the seams toward the triangle. Trim and square the corners, allowing a ½" seam allowance on the short ends for attaching the ruffle.

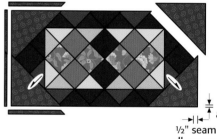

¼" seam allowance
½" seam allowance

4. Pin and sew 4¼" x 26½" pieces of fabric A to the pillow top and bottom. Press the seam allowances toward the border.

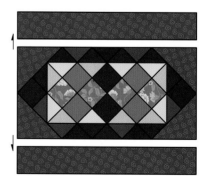

5. Layer the bordered block with a 22" x 28" piece of batting and a 22"x 28" piece of scrap backing. Baste the layers together.
6. Quilt the block matching the design used on the "Stepping Stones" quilt, or choose a quilting design that highlights the pieced center block.

7. Sew a ⅛" seam allowance around the outside of the pillow sham through all 3 layers. Trim the excess batting and scrap backing to match the block.

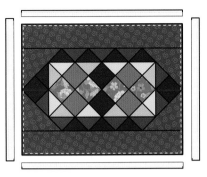

Baste and trim.

Pillow Sham Ruffle

1. Sew six 8"-wide ruffle strips end to end to create 1 continuous length. This will result in a large "tube" or "ring" of fabric. Press the seams open.
2. If you want to use fusible interfacing to stiffen or add more body to the ruffles, iron 4"-wide interfacing strips onto the wrong side of half of the ruffle fabric's 8" width.
3. Fold the ruffle in half wrong sides together. Press.
4. Use a basting stitch to sew ¼" inside the raw edges of the ruffle.
5. Pull the bobbin thread to create gathers until the ruffle is approximately 92" long.

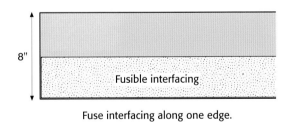

Fuse interfacing along one edge.

Press wrong sides together. Baste ¼" from raw edges.

Gather until ruffle is approximately 92" long.

6. Pin the gathered ruffle fabric around the outside of the pillow sham block, distributing the gathers evenly.
7. Baste the ruffle in place with a ¼" seam allowance.

Pillow Sham Back Assembly

1. Sew a 1" double-fold hem along the 21" edges of each backing piece. To do this, fold the raw edge over 1" and press; fold over 1" again and press. Stitch close to the inner edge.
2. Lay the smaller piece of backing fabric right sides together on the top of the pillow sham front; align the double-fold hem edge in the center of the pillow sham front. Take care to tuck the ruffle in toward the center of the pillow sham front. Pin into place.
3. Lay the second backing piece on top of the first, overlapping the hemmed edge 5". Pin into place.
4. Sew the layers together along the outside edges of the pillow sham front using a ½" seam allowance.

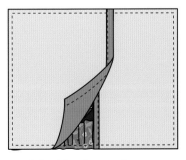

Stitch with ½" seam allowance.

5. Turn the pillow sham right side out. Insert a pillow.

Rose Garden Ensemble

Rose Wreath

Garden Path

Quilts by Pamela Lindquist, 88" x 108".
Machine quilted by Kris Bizzarri.

Who can resist a bouquet of large magnificent roses? In this quilt design the appliquéd rose stems interlace the pieced Rose blocks to create a wreath medallion. The rotary-cut pattern pieces use color gradation to add complexity to the block's appearance without complicating the assembly. Combining touches of simple appliquéd leaves and stems adds a graceful softness to the large, bold Rose blocks. The twisted ribbon border finishes the look of old fashioned charm. This quilt was designed to be the quilt top for this ensemble; the "Garden Path" quilt, shown above right, was designed as the back. Instructions for the "Rose Wreath" quilt begin on page 46. If you would like to make the coordinating "Rose Wreath" decorator pillows, see page 55 for additional yardage requirements.

A garden path is an invitation to explore the sights, sounds, and smells of the out-of-doors. Following a garden path, whether it be straight and narrow or long and winding, elicits a sense of discovery as well as a focus to our direction as we walk along. So it is with this quilt pattern. When done in florals, the simple symmetry and geometric design create a feeling of solid comfort, pleasing the eye and relaxing the soul. This quilt was designed to be the quilt back for the "Rose Wreath" quilt, shown above left. The "Garden Path" quilt top will be larger (91½" x 115½") than "Rose Wreath". You will trim it after quilting to match the size of "Rose Wreath." Instructions for the "Garden Path" quilt begin on page 51. If you want to make the coordinating pillow shams, see page 59 for yardage requirements.

"Rose Wreath" Quilt

Materials and Cutting

Yardage is based on 42"-wide fabric; strips are cut 42" long unless otherwise stated.

Fabric	Color and Value	Yardage	Strip Width	No. to Cut	Crosscut from Strips	Size
Fabric A* Roses	Assorted values of pink	½ yd. total	2½"	3	48 squares	2½" x 2½"
			2⅞"	2	24 squares	2⅞" x 2⅞" ◻
Fabric B** Background	Light print	4½ yds.	2½"	8	124 squares	2½" x 2½"
			2⅞"	2	24 squares	2⅞" x 2⅞" ◻
			12½"	3	1 square	12½" x 12½"
					2 rectangles	12½" x 32½"
					1 rectangle	12½" x 22½" piece
			22½"	3	2 rectangles	22½" x 32½"
					3 rectangles	22½" x 12½"
Ribbon border			2⅞"	2	23 squares	2⅞" x 2⅞" ◻
Fabric C Stems	Dark green print or solid	¼ yd.	1⅛" bias strips*	16	16 strips	1⅛" x 10"
Fabric D Leaves	Medium green prints	⅜ yd. total	–	–	24 leaves	Template pattern on page 50.
Fabric E Ribbon border	Medium green print	4¼ yds.	2⅞"	2	25 squares	2⅞" x 2⅞" ◻
Outer border			14½"	9	–	–
Fabric F Ribbon border	Dark green print	⅜ yd.	2½"	3	46 squares	2½" x 2½"
Fabric G Ribbon border	Medium pink print	¾ yd.	2½"	3	46 squares	2½" x 2½"
			2⅞"	4	44 squares	2⅞" x 2⅞" ◻
Backing***		8 yds.	–	–	–	–
Binding	Medium or dark green print	¾ yds.	2"	10	–	–
Batting		92" x 112" piece	–	–	–	–
Fusible Web (optional)		1 yd., 17" wide	–	–	–	–

* See "Before You Cut" on the opposite page.

** For best results, choose a subtle print that is non-directional. If you use a directional print, purchase an extra ½ yard and be sure to cut all the background pieces so that the design of the fabric will go the same way.

*** Backing fabric needed for non-reversible quilt only.

◻ Cut squares diagonally once.

Quilt size: 88" x 108"

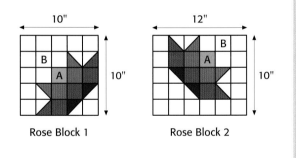

Rose Block 1   Rose Block 2

Before You Cut

When cutting the rose blocks, you may want to use a lighter color for the rose center square and have the colors become darker as they expand out to the base of the rose. (See the block illustration.) Hand-dyed fabrics in color gradations would be perfect for this. For 8 rose blocks, cut 8 light 2½" squares for the center, 16 medium and 24 dark 2½" squares. Cut 8 light to medium 2⅞" squares and 16 dark 2⅞" squares.

For help on cutting bias strips, see page 31 ("Blooming Baskets" quilt).

Rose Block Construction

1. Lay out the fabric A and fabric B squares and triangles matching the block diagrams.

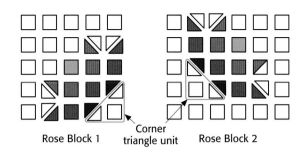

Rose Block 1   Corner triangle unit   Rose Block 2

2. **Rose block 1:** Sew the fabric A and B triangles together except for the fabric B pieces at the base of the rose labeled "corner triangle unit." Press the seam allowances toward the darker color.

3. Sew the squares into rows. Press the seam allowances in opposite directions from row to row.
4. Sew the rows together. Press the seam allowances in one direction.
5. Assemble the corner triangle unit and sew it to the main body of the Rose block. Press the seam open. (Attaching the corner triangle unit to the block as a separate unit will make it easier to open the seam when it is time to tuck the raw ends of the appliqué stems to the back of the quilt.) Make 4 blocks.

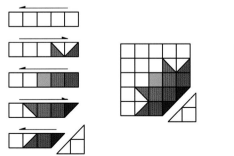

Rose Block 1
Make 4.

6. **Rose block 2:** Sew Rose block 2 in the same way as Rose block 1, but treat the side and bottom rows of fabric B as separate units as shown. Once the rose is pieced, attach the side and the bottom rows to complete the block. Make 4 blocks.

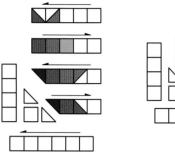 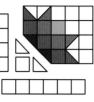

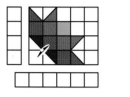

Rose Block 2

Wreath Medallion Assembly

1. Arrange the 8 Rose blocks around the center 12½" square of fabric B as shown.
2. Sew the blocks together to create rows. Press the seam allowances in opposite directions from row to row. Sew the rows together. Press the seam allowances in one direction.

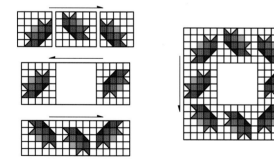

Preparing the Appliqué Shapes

1. **Stems:** Fold the fabric C bias stem strip in half wrong sides together. Sew ⅛" from the raw edges.

2. Roll the raw edge of the stem fabric to the back of the strip so it will be the "wrong side" when the stem is appliquéd onto the quilt.

⅛" seam allowance

3. **Leaves:** Make a template for the leaves from the pattern on page 50. Choose your favorite method of appliqué: hand, machine, or fusible.
4. Trace around the templates to make 24 leaves from assorted green fabric scraps or from the 3½" strip of fabric D. Add a scant ¼" seam allowance to each leaf shape as you cut it out if needed for your appliqué technique.

Appliquéing the Leaves and Stems

1. Refer to the diagram below and the photo on page 45 for placement of the stems and leaves. Pin the bias stems and 8 inner leaves to the center medallion. You will appliqué the leaves around the outside of the wreath later.
2. Appliqué the stems and the leaves to the quilt.
3. Make a small opening in the seam wherever the bias stem meets the rose. Insert the raw edge of the stem into the opened seam and re-sew the seam closed.

Completing the Quilt Center

1. Sew the 12½" x 32½" fabric B pieces to the sides of the center medallion; press the seam allowances away from the center.
2. Sew the 12½" x 22½" fabric B pieces to the sides of the 22½" x 32½" fabric B pieces. Press the seam allowances toward the center pieces.
3. Sew the top and the bottom pieces to the center medallion; press the seam allowances away from the center.
4. Pin remaining appliqué leaves into place and sew.

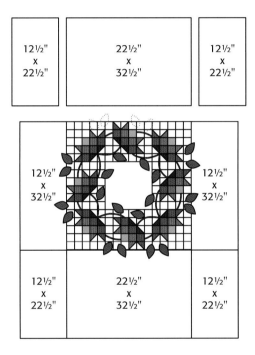

Twisted Ribbon Border

To create the twisted ribbon border, you will sew units and then join them together. Border units 1 and 2, border units 3 and 4, and the border end units are mirror images of each other. Pay close attention to the illustrations for correct placement and the total number of units to make. Follow the arrows for pressing direction.

1. To create border units 1 and 2, sew fabric B and E triangles to the fabric F squares. Press the seams all in one direction.

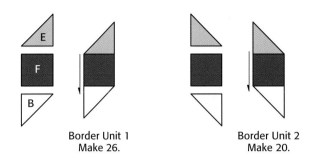

Border Unit 1
Make 26.

Border Unit 2
Make 20.

2. To create border units 3 and 4, sew fabric G triangles to fabric G squares. Press seams in the opposite direction of border units 1 and 2.

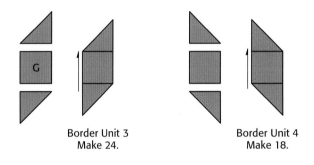

Border Unit 3
Make 24.

Border Unit 4
Make 18.

3. To create border end units, sew fabric E and G triangles to fabric G squares. Press.

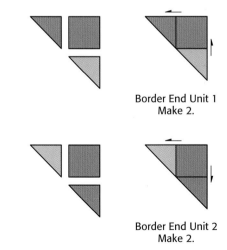

Border End Unit 1
Make 2.

Border End Unit 2
Make 2.

4. Starting with the left side of the quilt, alternate 13 border unit 1 sections and 12 border unit 3 sections referring to the quilt diagram below. Sew the units together. Press the seams in one direction being careful not to stretch the border.
5. Repeat step 4 for the right side of the quilt.
6. For the top border, alternate 10 border unit 2 sections and 9 border unit 4 sections. Sew and press as above.
7. Repeat step 6 for the bottom border.
8. Attach the border end units to the corners.

Attaching the Twisted Ribbon Border

The quilt center was cut larger than necessary to accommodate the fitting of the pieced border. Pieced borders have a tendency to stretch as you work on them, so handle them carefully.

1. Compare the lengths of your side ribbon border units to each other; compare the top and bottom borders. Their measurements should be the same.
2. Measure the quilt length and width through the center. Trim the quilt as needed so that the borders will fit perfectly.
3. Pin and sew the borders onto the quilt center matching the border end units and stitching a mitered seam.

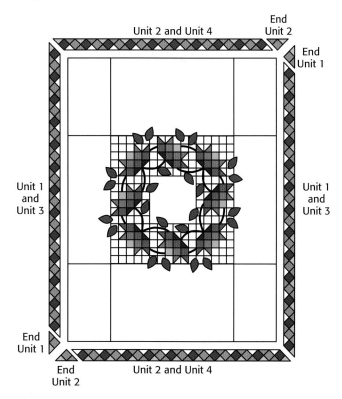

Outer Borders

1. Sew together the 14½"-wide outer-border strips to make 1 long strip of fabric.
2. Measure the length of the quilt through the center. Cut 2 border strips to that length. Pin and sew the border strips to the quilt sides. Press the seam allowances toward the outer border.
3. Measure the width of the quilt through the center. Cut 2 border strips to that length. Pin and sew the borders to the quilt top and bottom. Press the seams toward the outer border.

Quilt Finishing

Refer to "Finishing Your Quilt" on pages 6–8.

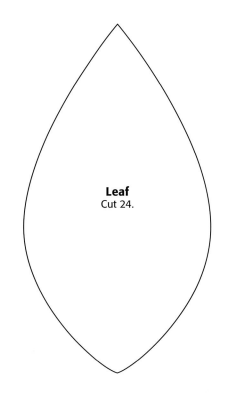

Leaf
Cut 24.

"Garden Path" Quilt

Materials and Cutting

Yardage is based on 42"-wide fabric; all strips are cut 42" long unless otherwise stated.

Fabric	Color and Value	Yardage	Strip Width	No. to Cut	Crosscut from Strips	Size
Fabric A Four-patch units	Medium pink floral print	2 yds.	2½"	24	–	–
Fabric B Four-patch units	Light green floral print	2 yds.	2½"	24	–	–
Fabric C Half-square-triangle units	Dark green print or solid	1¾ yds.	4⅞"	11	82 squares	4⅞"
Fabric D* Half-square-triangle units	Light to medium green print or solid	1¾ yds.	4⅞"	11	82 squares	4⅞"
Inner Border	Dark green solid	⅝ yd.	2"	8	–	–
Outer Border*	Light to medium green print or solid	3⅝ yds.	12½"	9	–	–
Backing**		8½ yds.	–	–	–	–
Binding	Light to medium green print	¾ yd.	2"	11	–	–
Batting		96" x 120" piece	–	–	–	–

* If you want the half-square triangles and the outer border to be of the same fabric, you will need 5⅜ yards.

** Backing fabric needed for non-reversible quilt only.

Quilt size: 91" x 115"
Block 1 finished size: 12" x 12"
Block 2 finished size: 12" x 12"
Block 3 finished size: 8" x 12"
Block 4 finished size: 8" x 12"
Block 5 finished size: 12" x 8"
Block 6 finished size: 12" x 8"
Block 7 finished size: 8" x 8"
Block 8 finished size: 8" x 8"

Block Construction

This quilt is constructed of blocks made from a number of the same units sewn into different configurations. The two units used are a four-patch unit and a half-square-triangle unit.

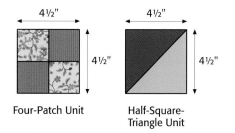

Four-Patch Unit   Half-Square-Triangle Unit

1. **Four-patch unit:** Sew the 2½"-wide strips of fabric A and fabric B together in pairs as shown below to make 24 strip sets. Press the seam allowances toward the darker fabric.

Make 24 strip sets.

2. Cut the strip sets into 376 segments, each 2½" wide.

Cut 376.

3. Sew the segments together to make 188 four-patch units measuring 4½" square. Press the seams open.

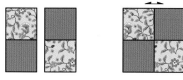

Make 188.

4. **Half-square-triangle unit:** Layer the 4⅞" squares of fabric C and fabric D in pairs with right sides together. Cut diagonally in half once. Keep the triangles layered together in pairs.

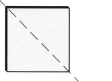

5. Stitch together the pairs of fabric C and fabric D triangles, sewing along the diagonal. Press toward the darker fabric. Make 164 half-square-triangle units measuring 4½" square.

Make 164.

Block Assembly

1. Using the illustrations below as a guide, arrange the four-patch units and the half-square-triangle units to create the correct number of blocks.

2. To assemble the blocks, first sew the units together by rows. Press the seam allowances in opposite directions from row to row. Sew the rows together. Press the seam allowances in one direction.

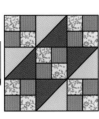

Block 1
Make 12.

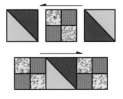
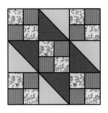

Block 2
Make 12.

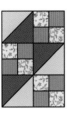

Block 3
Make 6.

Block 4
Make 6.

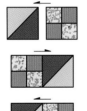
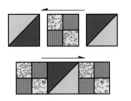

Block 5
Make 4.

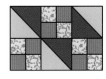

Block 6
Make 4.

Block 7
Make 2.

Block 8
Make 2.

Quilt-Top Assembly

Arrange the pieced blocks as shown in the assembly diagram. Sew the blocks together to create rows. Press the seam allowances in opposite directions from row to row. Sew the rows together. Press the seam allowances in one direction.

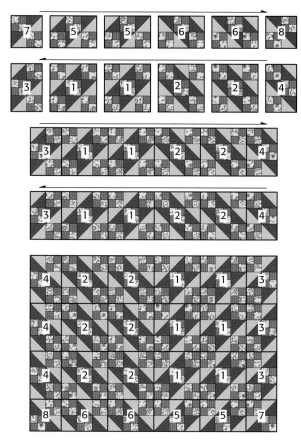

Assembly Diagram

Borders

1. Join the strips for the inner border from end to end to make 1 continuous strip of fabric.
2. Measure the length of the quilt top through the center. From the continuous strip, cut 2 borders to that length. Pin and sew the borders to the sides of the quilt top. Press the seam allowances toward the borders.
3. Measure the width of the quilt top through the center. From the continuous strip, cut 2 borders to that length. Pin and sew the borders to the top and bottom of the quilt top. Press the seam allowances toward the borders.
4. Repeat steps 1 through 3 for the outer border.

Quilt Finishing

Refer to "Finishing Your Quilt" on pages 6–8.

"Rose Wreath" Decorator Pillows

Materials and Cutting for 2 Decorator Pillows

Yardage is based on 42"-wide fabric; strips are cut 42" long unless otherwise stated.

Fabric	Color and Value	Yardage	Strip Width	No. to Cut	Crosscut from Strips	Size
Fabric A Roses	Light, medium, and dark pinks	¼ yd. total	2½"	1	12 squares	2½" x 2½"
			2⅞"	1	6 squares	2⅞" x 2⅞" ◻
Fabric B Background	Light print	⅝ yd.	2½"	5	74 squares	2½" x 2½"
			2⅞"	1	6 squares	2⅞" x 2⅞" ◻
Fabric C Stems	Dark green print or solid	1 fat quarter	1⅛" bias cut	2	2 strips	1⅛" x 23"
Fabric D Leaves	Medium green prints	⅛ yd. total	–	–	4 leaves	Template pattern on page 50.
Piping	Medium pink print	¼ yd.	1"	4	8 strips	1" x 14½"
Border	Dark green print	¼ yd.	1½"	4	4 strips	1½" x 14½"
					4 strips	1½" x 16½"
Flange	Light to medium green print	1 yd.	3½"	8	8 strips	3½" x 22½"
Scrap Backing		Two 18" x 18" squares	–	–	–	–
Backing	Light to medium green print	1½ yds.	22½"	2	2 rectangles	13½" x 22½"
					2 rectangles	16½" x 22½"
Batting		Two 18" x 18" squares	–	–	–	–
Fusible Interfacing (optional)		⅞ yd.	3½"	4	4 strips	3½" x 23"
Tissue Paper or Tracing Paper		–	–	–	–	–

◻ *Cut squares once diagonally.*

These pillows are companions for the "Rose Wreath" quilt on page 47. Use the same or very similar fabrics to that used in the quilt for the best results.

Finished size: 22" x 22"
Fits a standard 16" x 16" pillow form

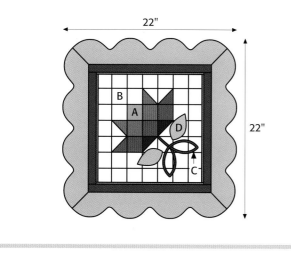

Pillow Front Assembly
(Instructions for 1 Pillow)

1. Follow the directions beginning with "Rose Block Construction" on page 47 to make Rose block 1.
2. Arrange the Rose block and 2½" squares of fabric B as shown below.

3. Sew the 2½" squares of fabric B into rows. Press the seam allowances in one direction. Attach the fabric B rows onto the Rose block. Press the seam allowances in one direction.

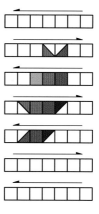
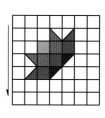

4. Follow the directions in "Preparing the Appliqué Shapes" on page 48 to make a bias stem from a 23" long fabric C bias strip.
5. Using the template pattern on page 50, cut out 2 leaves from fabric D.
6. Refer to the illustration below and position the bias stem and the leaves in place on the background.
7. Appliqué the stem and leaves to the pieced block; open up the seam allowance to tuck the stem end under the pieced rose.

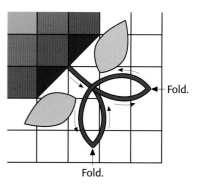

8. Fold four 1"-wide strips of piping fabric in half lengthwise with wrong sides together and press. Sew 1 strip to each side of the "Rose" block, matching the raw edges of the piping strip with the raw edges of the block. Use a ⅛" seam

allowance. Press flat; do not flip the piping back toward the seam allowance.

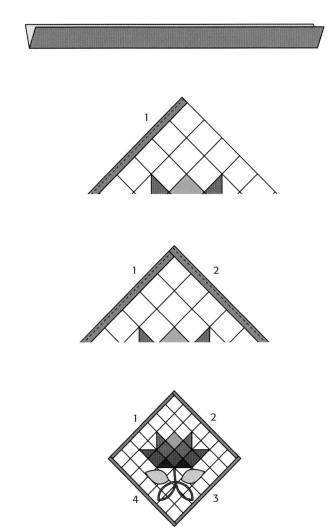

9. Pin and sew 1½" x 14½" borders to the Rose block sides. Press the seam allowances toward the borders. Pin and sew 1½" x 16½" borders to the top and bottom. Press the seam allowances toward the borders.

10. Layer the bordered block with an 18" x 18" piece of batting and an 18" x 18" piece of scrap backing. Baste the layers together. Quilt the block matching the pattern used on the "Rose Wreath" quilt, or choose a pattern that highlights the pieced rose.

11. Sew a ⅛" seam allowance around the outside of the bordered pillow block through all 3 layers. Trim the excess batting and scrap backing even with the edges of the bordered block.

Pillow Flanges

1. With right sides together, center one of the 22½"-long strips along the top of the pillow block. Sew the strip onto the pillow block starting ¼" in from the edge of the pillow block and stopping ¼" from the edge of the pillow block. Press the seam allowances toward the border.

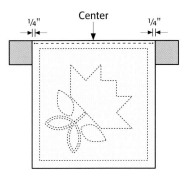

2. Repeat step 1 to sew three of the remaining flange strips to the pillow block.

3. Lay the pillow block right side up on a flat surface. At each corner, fold one of the borders under at a 45° angle. Adjust the fold until the seams meet to make a mitered corner. Pin in place. Place a transparent square ruler over each corner to check the angle. Press the folded corners. Sew the seams by hand. Trim the fabric

from the back leaving a ⅜" seam allowance. Press the seams open.

4. Use the curve patterns on page 62 as a guide for making the curved edges. Cut 4 pieces of tissue paper or tracing paper to 3½" x 23". Trace the curves for the sides and corners onto each piece of paper.

5. Pin the tracing-paper pattern sections onto the flanges, making sure the curved lines touch the outside edge of the flanges. Adjust the pattern as necessary to create gentle curves, using a marking pen to draw smooth connecting curve lines on the tracing paper. Tape the sections together if desired. Cut the curves out of the fabric.

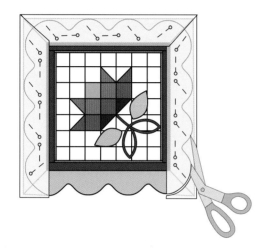

Pillow Back Assembly

1. Make a 1" double-fold hem along a 22½" edge of each pillow back. To do this, fold over 1" and press; fold over 1" again and press. Stitch close to the inner folded edge.

2. Lay the smaller backing fabric on top of the pillow front with right sides together and aligning the double-fold-hem edge with the center of the pillow. Pin into place.

3. Lay the second piece of backing fabric on the pillow front with right sides together. Overlap the hemmed edge 3". Pin into place. Secure the backing fabrics in place with just enough pins to be able to flip the pillow sham over to the front side. *Note:* If you are using fusible interfacing to stiffen and add body to the flanges, lay the 4 strips on the pillow backing. Cut the ends of the interfacing strips to meet at 45° angles at the corners. Cut the top and bottom strips so they

butt against the hemmed edges. Iron the strips along the outside edges of the pillow back, according to the manufacturer's directions.

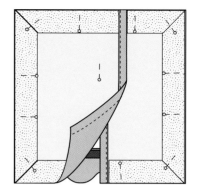

4. Flip the pillow sham over. Pin the top onto the bottom pieces. Remove pins on the back side.

5. Sew a ¼" seam allowance along the curved edge. Remove the pins.

6. Using the curved stitching as a guide, trim the excess fabric to create a ¼" seam allowance. Clip the curves and turn the pillow to the right side. Press the border.

7. From the pillow top, sew along the inside border seam through all layers to create the flange.

8. Insert the pillow form.

"Garden Path" Pillow Shams

Materials and Cutting for 2 Pillow Shams

Yardage is based on 42"-wide fabric; all strips are cut 42" long unless otherwise stated.

Fabric	Color and Value	Yardage	Strip Width	No. to Cut	Crosscut from Strips	Size
Fabric A Four-patch units	Medium pink floral print	¼ yd.	2½"	1	–	–
Fabric B Four-patch units	Light green floral print	¼ yd.	2½"	1	–	–
Fabric C Half-square-triangle-units and Border	Dark green print or solid	1 yd.	4⅞" 4½" 5½" 2½"	1 1 2 4	8 squares 8 squares 4 rectangles 4 strips	4⅞" x 4⅞" 4½" x 4½" 5½" x 16½" 2½" x 26½"
Fabric D Half-square-triangle units and flange	Light to medium green print or solid	1¼ yds.	4⅞" 4"	1 8	8 squares 4 strips 4 strips	4⅞" x 4⅞" 4" x 34" 4" x 28"
Scrap Backing		Two 22" x 28" pieces	–	–	–	–
Backing	Medium green	2⅜ yd.	27½" 24"	1 2	2 rectangles 2 rectangles	19" x 28" 24" x 28"
Batting		Two 22" x 28" pieces	–	–	–	–
Fusible Interfacing (optional)		1⅞ yd.	–	–	4 strips 4 strips	4" x 34" 4" x 28"
Tissue Paper or Tracing Paper		–	–	–	–	–

These pillow shams are designed to be companions for the "Garden Path" quilt on page 52. Use the same or similar fabrics as were used in the quilt; you can add some fabrics from your stash as well.

Finished size: 27" x 33"
Fits a standard 20" x 26" bed pillow

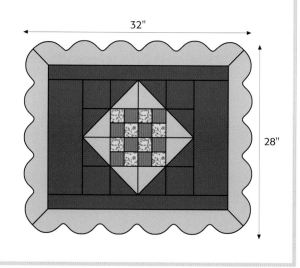

Pillow Sham Front Assembly
(Instructions for 1 Sham)

1. Follow the directions on page 52 to make 4 four-patch units. Use the 2½"-wide strips of fabrics A and B.

2. Follow the directions on page 52 to make 8 half-square-triangle units. Use the 4⅞" squares of fabrics C and D.

3. Arrange the four-patch units, the half-square-triangle units, and the 4½" fabric C squares as shown in the pillow sham diagram below.

4. Sew the units together in rows. Press the seam allowances in opposite directions from row to row. Sew the rows together. Press the seam allowances in one direction.

5. Pin and sew 5½"-wide fabric C borders to the pillow sides. Press the seam allowances toward the border.

6. Pin and sew 2½"-wide fabric C borders to the pillow top and bottom. Press the seam allowances toward the border.

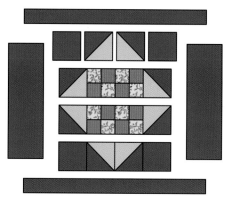

7. Layer the pillow top with a 22" x 28" piece of batting and scrap backing. Baste the layers together.

8. Quilt the block matching the pattern used on the "Garden Path" quilt or choose a pattern that highlights the pieced center block.

9. Sew a ⅛" seam allowance around the outside of the pillow sham through all 3 layers. Trim the excess batting and scrap backing even with the pillow sham top.

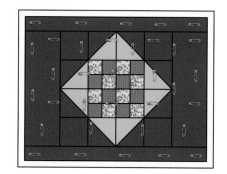

Pillow Flanges

1. With right sides together, center a 4" x 34" flange strip along the top of the pillow sham block. Sew the strip onto the pillow sham starting ¼" in from the edge of the pillow sham block and stopping ¼" from the edge. Press the seam allowances toward the border.

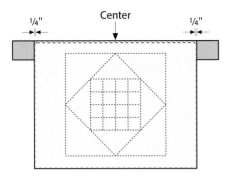

2. Repeat step 1 to sew three of the remaining flange strips to the pillow sham.

3. Lay the pillow sham block right side up on a flat surface. Fold one of the borders under at a 45° angle. Adjust the fold until the seams meet to make a mitered corner. Pin into place. Place a transparent square ruler over the corner to check the angle. Press the folded corner. Sew the seam by hand. Trim the excess fabric leaving a ⅜" seam allowance. Press the seams open.

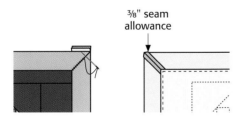

⅜" seam allowance

4. Use the curve patterns on page 62 as a guide for making the curved edges. Cut 2 pieces of tissue paper or tracing paper 4" x 34", and 2 pieces 4" x 28". Trace the curves for the sides and corners onto each piece of paper.

5. Pin the tracing-paper pattern sections onto the flanges making sure the curved lines touch the outside edge of the flanges. Adjust the pattern as necessary to create gentle curves, using a marking pen to draw smooth connecting curve lines

on the tracing paper. Tape the sections together if desired. Cut the curves out of the fabric.

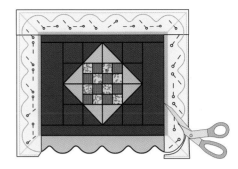

Pillow Sham Back Assembly

1. Make a 1" double-fold hem along one of the 28" edges of each backing piece. To do this, fold over 1" and press; fold over 1" again and press. Stitch close to the inner fold.

2. Lay the smaller backing fabric piece right sides together on the top of the pillow sham front aligning the hemmed edge with the center of the pillow sham. Pin into place.

3. Lay the second piece of backing fabric right side down on top of the first; overlap the hemmed edge 5". Pin into place. Secure the backing fabrics with just enough pins to be able to flip the pillow sham over to the front side.

4. Flip the pillow sham over. Pin the top onto the bottom pieces. Remove pins on the back side. *Note:* If you are using fusible interfacing to stiffen and add body to the flange, place the strips along the outside edges of the pillow sham back. Cut the ends of the strips to meet at 45° angles at the corners. Cut the top and bottom strips so they butt up against the hemmed edges. Iron the strips, following the manufacturer's instructions.

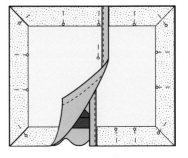

5. Sew a ¼" seam allowance along the curved edge. Remove the pins.

6. Trim the excess fabric. Clip the curves and turn the pillow sham to the right side. Press the border.

7. From the pillow top, sew along the inside border seam through all layers to create the flange.

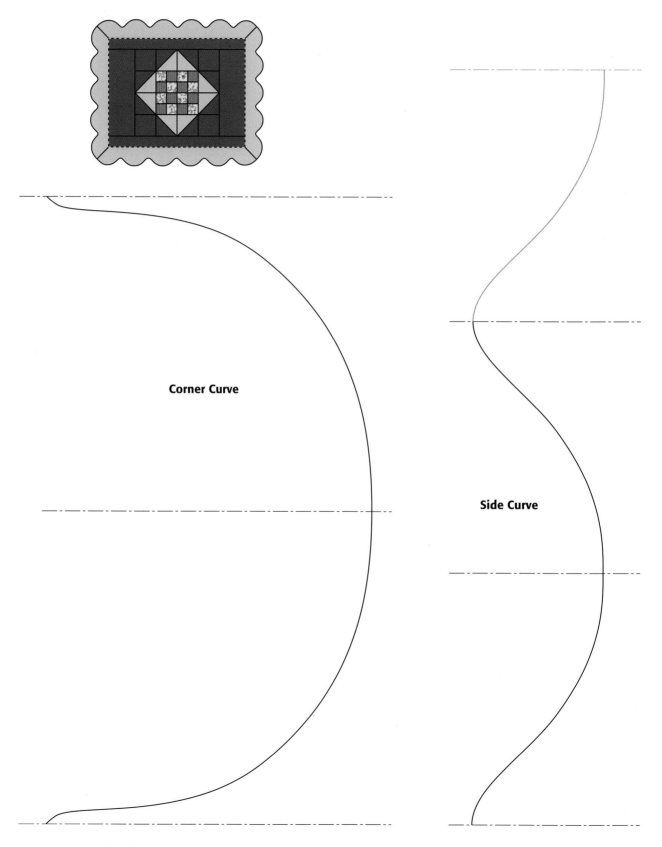

Corner Curve

Side Curve

Bibliography

Pahl, Ellen, ed. *The Quilters Ultimate Visual Guide.* Emmaus, Penn.: Rodale Press, 1997.

Simplicity Pattern Company, Inc. *Simplicity's Simply the Best Home Decorating Book.* New York: Simon & Schuster, 1993.

Wolfrom, Joen. *Make Any Block Any Size.* Concord, Calif.: C & T Publishing, 1999.

About the Author

Pamela Lindquist is a self-taught seamstress with over thirty years of sewing experience, having sewn quilts as gifts for family and friends. Needlework and sewing have been an important form of personal expression and relaxation for Pam since she was a child. For a while, school, career, and family kept her busy and away from serious quilting projects. Her interest was rekindled when her twenty-five-year-old sewing machine, a high school graduation gift, needed replacing. While shopping for a new machine, she discovered new quilt designs, construction techniques, and tools that rekindled her interest in quilting. Pam lives in Eugene, Oregon, with her husband and two teenage children.

new and bestselling titles from

America's Best-Loved Craft & Hobby Books™

America's Best-Loved Quilt Books®

NEW RELEASES
Bear's Paw Plus
All through the Woods
American Quilt Classics
Amish Wall Quilts
Animal Kingdom CD-ROM
Batik Beauties
The Casual Quilter
Fantasy Floral Quilts
Fast Fusible Quilts
Friendship Blocks
From the Heart
Log Cabin Fever
Machine-Stitched Cathedral Stars
Magical Hexagons
Potting Shed Patchwork
Quilts from Larkspur Farm
Repliqué Quilts
Successful Scrap Quilts
   from Simple Rectangles

APPLIQUÉ
Artful Album Quilts
Artful Appliqué
Colonial Appliqué
Red and Green: An Appliqué Tradition
Rose Sampler Supreme

BABY QUILTS
Easy Paper-Pieced Baby Quilts
Even More Quilts for Baby: Easy as ABC
More Quilts for Baby: Easy as ABC
Play Quilts
The Quilted Nursery
Quilts for Baby: Easy as ABC

HOLIDAY QUILTS
Christmas at That Patchwork Place
Holiday Collage Quilts
Paper Piece a Merry Christmas
A Snowman's Family Album Quilt
Welcome to the North Pole

LEARNING TO QUILT
Basic Quiltmaking Techniques for:
   Borders and Bindings
   Divided Circles
   Hand Appliqué
   Machine Appliqué
   Strip Piecing
The Joy of Quilting
The Simple Joys of Quilting
Your First Quilt Book (or it should be!)

PAPER PIECING
50 Fabulous Paper-Pieced Stars
For the Birds
Paper Piece a Flower Garden
Paper-Pieced Bed Quilts
Paper-Pieced Curves
A Quilter's Ark
Show Me How to Paper Piece

ROTARY CUTTING
101 Fabulous Rotary-Cut Quilts
365 Quilt Blocks a Year Perpetual Calendar
Around the Block Again
Biblical Blocks
Creating Quilts with Simple Shapes
Flannel Quilts
More Fat Quarter Quilts
More Quick Watercolor Quilts
Razzle Dazzle Quilts

SCRAP QUILTS
Nickel Quilts
Scrap Frenzy
Scrappy Duos
Spectacular Scraps

CRAFTS
The Art of Stenciling
Baby Dolls and Their Clothes
Creating with Paint
The Decorated Kitchen
The Decorated Porch
A Handcrafted Christmas
Painted Chairs
Sassy Cats

KNITTING & CROCHET
Too Cute!
Clever Knits
Crochet for Babies and Toddlers
Crocheted Sweaters
Fair Isle Sweaters Simplified
Irresistible Knits
Knit It Your Way
Knitted Shawls, Stoles, and Scarves
Knitted Sweaters for Every Season
Knitting with Novelty Yarns
Paintbox Knits
Simply Beautiful Sweaters
Simply Beautiful Sweaters for Men
The Ultimate Knitter's Guide

Our books are available at bookstores and your favorite craft, fabric and yarn retailers. If you don't see the title you're looking for, visit us at www.martingale-pub.com or contact us at:

1-800-426-3126

International: 1-425-483-3313

Fax: 1-425-486-7596

E-mail: info@martingale-pub.com

For more information and a full list of our titles, visit our Web site or call for a free catalog.
